The Sanford Meisner Approach

WORKBOOK FOUR
playing the part

Smith and Kraus *Books For Actors*

CAREER DEVELOPMENT: Technique
Acting Under the Circumstances: Variations on a Theme of Stanislavski,
    A Step-by-Step Approach to Playing a Part
The Actor's Chekhov
All the Words on Stage
The Great Acting Teachers and Their Methods
Head First Acting: Exercises for High-School Drama Students
In Other Words: Women Directors Speak
The Sanford Meisner Approach Workbook I: An Actor's Workbook
The Sanford Meisner Approach Workbook II: Emotional Freedom
The Sanford Meisner Approach Workbook III: Tackling the Text
Taken to the Stage: The Education of an Actress by Mimi Kennedy
TIPS: Ideas for Actors
TIPS: Ideas for Directors
Toward Mastery: An Acting Class with Nikos Psacharopoulos

CAREER DEVELOPMENT: Auditioning
Auditioning for the Musical Theatre
The Camera Smart Actor
Hot Tips for Cold Readings: Some Do's and Don'ts for Actors at Auditions
Loving to Audition The Audition Workbook
The Ultimate Monologue Index 2nd Edition

CAREER DEVELOPMENT: Actors Guides
The Actor's Guide to Qualified Acting Coaches: Los Angeles
The Actor's Guide to Qualified Acting Coaches: New York
How to Produce a Play Without a Producer: A Survival Guide for Actors and
    Playwrights
The Job Book: 100 Acting Jobs for Actors
The Job Book II: 100 Day Jobs for Actors
What To Give Your Agent For Christmas and 100 Other Tips for the Working
    Actor

If you require prepublication information about upcoming Smith and Kraus
books, you may receive our semiannual catalogue, free of charge, by sending
your name and address to *Smith and Kraus Catalogue, P.O. Box 127, Lyme,
NH 03768. Or call us at (800) 895-4331, fax (603) 643-1831.*

The Sanford Meisner Approach

WORKBOOK FOUR
playing the part

Larry Silverberg

Career Development Series

A SMITH AND KRAUS BOOK

Published by Smith and Kraus, Inc.
177 Lyme Road, Hanover, NH 03755
www.smithkraus.com

Copyright ©2000 by Larry Silverberg

Manufactured in the United States of America
Cover and Text Design by Julia Hill Gignoux

First Edition: June 2000
10 9 8 7 6 5 4 3 2 1

The Library of Congress Cataloging-In-Publication Data

Silverberg, Larry, 1959–
The Sanford Meisner approach: workbook four: playing the part /
by Larry Silverberg.

p. cm. (A career development book)
ISBN 1-57525-212-0

1. Drama—Explication. 2. Meisner, Sanford. I. Title.
PN1707.S46   1998
808.2–dc21   98-23061
CIP

acknowledgments

For this, my fourth book on the Meisner Approach, I want to say a very special thank you to Horton Foote who, as you will see, plays a starring role on the following pages. Thank you Horton for your generosity and friendship and for allowing me to include your play, *A Young Lady of Property*, as the inspiration for the lessons of interpretation in this book.

Without my wonderful, brilliant teacher, my dear friend, Suzanne Shepherd, this book would have been impossible. Suzanne's voice, her heart and spirit, live in everything I do as an actor and teacher and I am deeply indebted to her. I love you Suzanne!

I thank my dear friend April Shawhan for her continual support. Through some difficult times during the writing of this book, April helped me keep going. I have learned so much about being fully human – on stage and off – from April and I love her very much.

I am deeply grateful to a very dear Frances Sternhagen for accepting my invitation to write the preface for this book. Frances has been so generous and supportive to me and to my students, and having her be a part of this book is a real thrill! I will tell you more about Frances in the "wrap-up" chapter of this book.

I thank the students in my nine-month Meisner Actor's Training Program at the School for Film and Television in New York City. I am continually inspired by the courage and tenacity of my students and they are a gift in my life. I also think it would be fun for you to know that, although I have invented the scenes in which I work with the "students" in this book, the names I have used are the actual names of my current New York students.

I thank my publishers, Marisa and Eric, for their insights, wisdom, humor, for their friendship and for the warm glow of their spirit. When I had finished Meisner Approach book one, I said "Well, I guess I'll see ya around." They said, "No, you have some more books in you." I said, "I do?" They said, "Yes, give it some thought." I took their advice. That's how this four volume series came about.

Thank you to Julia Hill Gignoux for so lovingly designing my books and for being such a treat to work with!

I save my deepest gratitude for last, to the man who opened my eyes and heart in the most profound ways and to whose work I have devoted my adult life. Sandy, for me and for thousands of others, your lessons are a greater gift than you ever could have imagined and I thank you with all my heart.

*For Mom, Dad,
and Grandma Ethel*

playing the part
contents

preface

A lot of people these days think they want to be actors. The profusion of films and television shows makes it look so easy. Media hype can lift the performance of an actor in a good film way beyond "good"; suddenly he or she is the new Big Star with a lot of attention and a lot of money. Many people think, "I want that. I want to be an actor." But they have very little notion of what acting involves.

I studied with Sanford Meisner in the fifties — the Dark Ages to some young students, I'm sure. When I spotted Larry Silverberg's first book on the Sanford Meisner approach, I was skeptical: There are so many books on acting, and how can Sandy's teaching be learned from a book? So, I began to glance through it, and the first thing that struck me was the spirit of joy and generosity that emanated from almost every page. The next thing, of course, was that Larry had, indeed, absorbed Sandy's approach and knew how to put it on paper. Students who have studied or are studying the Meisner approach can be reminded and refreshed, and people who are unfamiliar with it can begin to understand the commitment and dedication required of an actor who loves the process, not just the result. I bought the book.

This fourth book is about what I love: working with the text of a play. The text is what an actor should start with and what an actor should end with. If you're in a play that you have to perform for months or maybe years (I was in *Driving Miss Daisy* for two and a half years and *The Heiress* for a year and a half), you must be able to keep the text fresh and personal for yourself so the audience gets its money's worth and you don't get bored or tired.

A playwright is not happy when actors change lines to suit themselves. ("Do I have to say this? I'm not comfortable saying this.") Tough. Those are the lines. If you're involved in the first production of a play, you may have some input as to line changes, or even speech changes, because theater is a collaborative venture. The playwright wants it to be as good as it can be. But even in early rehearsals of a new play, your job as an actor is to try the lines as written — many times, perhaps — before suggesting a change.

Actors who changes lines or blocking "to keep it fresh" don't usually know how to keep it fresh.

Larry's fourth book — on working with a text — helps the actor find a way to make the play and the character personal to the actor, and, using the same technique, to keep it fresh. He helps the actor find things in the actor's own emotional experience and imagination that correspond to what is happening to the character in the play.

The best playwrights have their own rhythm, and rhythm is very important. Rhythm helps make it easy to learn lines, and rhythm helps to keep the lines and the scene fresh. Sandy used to use the example of playing a musical instrument to illustrate the importance to an actor of practicing something over and over. I remember once hearing John Gielgud say that occasionally he wasn't sure what a speech in Shakespeare meant, but that if he said it over and over, the rhythm would convey the meaning to him — the emotional meaning.

When a director guides a group of actors in a play — choreographs it, if you will — much of what the director has done has to do with rhythm and pace. Therefore, maintaining the rhythm is vital to the performance. In an opera or a musical, the conductor keeps everyone in the right rhythm, but in a play, once the director has gone, the actors and the stage manager have to maintain the rhythm themselves. Good actors can maintain the rhythm of a play by keeping the inner life fresh — which is what Larry's fourth book is about.

I was a bit daunted when Larry asked me to introduce this book. I haven't been a student for a long time. But I do think he's made Sandy's approach to acting as clear and accessible as any book on acting that I've read, and his enthusiasm for what's real in life is heartwarming and infectious. Acting should be fun. Even the tragedies should be fun, a thrill to do. The process *is* fun, and Larry really makes it so.

Frances Sternhagen

Without passion
man is a mere latent force and possibility,
like the flint which awaits the shock of the iron
before it can give forth its spark.

Henri-Frédéric Amiel

What is passion? It is surely the becoming of a person. Are we not, for most of our lives, marking time? Most of our being is at rest, unlived. In passion, the body and the spirit seek expression outside of self. Passion is all that is other from self. Sex is only interesting when it releases passion. The more extreme and the more expressed that passion is, the more unbearable does life seem without it. It reminds us that if passion dies or is denied, we are partly dead and that soon, come what may, we will be wholly so.

John Boorman

introduction

Welcome. Playing the part, or "interpretation," the subject of this, the fourth book in my Meisner series, calls upon our individual creativity and inventiveness in ways we have not addressed yet. An intricate aspect of our craft, many actors never fully address interpretation for one simple reason — it's hard work. I want you to know that the tools I am going to give you here will have the most wonderful payoff in your struggle to bring "soul" to the stage.

Interpretation for the actor is an ever expanding process because there is no "one way," and because each time we face the challenge of bringing the character to life, we will be faced with entering the unknown, with investigating from every angle, with questioning and discovering anew.

Everything we have been working on together in my first three Meisner Approach books has been with the aim of leading you to a pure connection with your instinctual "voice," strengthening your actors imagination, and giving you the ability to work with deep personal meaning.

Now we will put all of these skills to use in a most active way. That's a key word for us, "active," because in each moment on stage, we must be on a quest, passionately fighting for what we believe is necessary and true. What, specifically, does that mean? Hold that question for now, as the answer will become clear as you work your way through this book.

Let's get to it.

Every man feels instinctively
that all the beautiful sentiments in the world
weigh less than a single lovely action.
James Russell Lowell

chapter one

the nursery rhyme exercise

I am going to begin our work together with an exercise I find very useful and a lot of fun. It is called the nursery rhyme exercise and it is mainly about one thing: It is about having the experience of justifying the words. To be simple, what this means is, the words you speak on stage must have a purpose. Another way of saying this is, words must always be spoken in order to accomplish something. This is equally true when you are not speaking because your nonverbal behavior must also be aimed at something specific you are trying to achieve.

Let's get very basic about this whole thing. A long time ago, I told you that acting is doing. I also told you that when you are not involved in something you are doing, you are no longer acting. In the early phase of our work together, I taught you how to do "activities" that were a physical manifestation of the acting truth that says: "In each moment on stage you must be trying to accomplish something which is specific and meaningful." Specific and meaningful to whom? Yes, to you. If I haven't said this to you before, I will tell you now that every word out of your mouth and every ounce of your behavior on stage is part of an "activity" because everything you do on stage must be your determined attempt to get closer to this thing you want to have or which you need to make happen.

The truth is, in each moment, you are doing this in your life as well. When you speak and when you are not speaking, you are trying to accomplish something with the people you are with. Although most of the time you don't stop to consciously consider what you are trying to accomplish, that doesn't mean it isn't happening. And, what you want to achieve in each encounter is both specific and personal. So, before we get to the nursery rhyme exercise, I want you to investigate what is really happening when you are with the people in your life.

Here are two writing assignments (please complete the first one before you move on to the second):

1. During the following twenty-four hours, bring to your awareness what you are trying to accomplish in one of your interactions. I am asking you to take some time after you have been with a friend or family member, or after you have spent some time with a stranger (talking with a sales person or with someone on line at the bank, etc.), and figure out what you wanted to achieve with that person. Write down what you discovered on the lines below.

_____

_____

_____

_____

_____

_____

_____

_____

_____

_____

_____

_____

_____

_____

_____

_____

_____

_____

_____

_____

_____

2. During the next twenty-four hours, after a specific interaction with someone, take some time to consider the words and the behavior of the person you were with. Write about what it was you think he or she was trying to achieve or accomplish with you.

_____
_____
_____
_____
_____
_____
_____
_____
_____
_____
_____
_____
_____
_____
_____
_____
_____
_____
_____
_____
_____
_____
_____
_____
_____
_____
_____

Let's move on to the nursery rhyme exercise. To introduce it to you, I want you to meet one of your classmates,
Celina.

Larry: Celina, would you please say hello to the readers?

Celina: *(Smiling and giggling a little, she pushes her
golden hair back from her eyes.)* Hi out there!

Here is the well-known nursery rhyme I assigned Celina
to work on:

Mary had a little lamb,
its fleece was white as snow.
And everywhere that Mary went,
the lamb was sure to go.

Before you, the readers, joined us, I explained to Celina
and the rest of my "in person" class, how to approach the
nursery rhyme exercise and I gave everyone some time to
get to work on them. Let's listen to how Celina has started
the work on her nursery rhyme. Here are the beginnings of
the scenario she has come up with:

Celina: The characters are Mom, Dad, Sally (eight years old)
and Billy (thirteen years old) and Mary (fifteen years
old). It is dinner time. As my play begins, Sally and Billy
are at the table picking at their food. Mom, humming a
tune to ease the tension in the room, is putting food
onto a serving tray. Dad, upset that Mary has not
returned for dinner, is standing at the door. Dad suddenly yells out the door, "MARY!" He then waits a
moment, watches, and quite displeased, heads back to
the table. Mom, meanwhile, has walked over with the

food to Billy and starts to put a piece of lamb on to his plate. Not fond of the first piece of lamb he wrestled with, he stops her with his fork and says, "Had a little." Mom continues on to Dad who is now sitting at his plate eating a potato. Mom begins to serve Dad a piece of meat. "Lamb?" she asks. Not looking up from the next potato he is slicing, Dad shakes his head refusing her offer. Mom then serves herself a piece of lamb and sits down to eat.

All right, let's examine what Celina did:

She created a play including both a story line and a cast of characters that have nothing to do with the story or the characters in the original nursery rhyme.

She took the words from the nursery rhyme and broke them down into "lines" for the characters in her play in such a way that each person who is speaking has a reason for saying those words. Also, did you notice that Celina used the words from the nursery rhyme in their exact order and she didn't change, add, or delete any words? If you go back and look, you will see that the original line "Mary had a little lamb" became her "script," which looks like this:

Dad: MARY!
Billy: Had a little.
Mom: Lamb?

Celina added sound that is not in the original nursery rhyme. What sound? She has the Mom humming. As with everything else, her humming is justified. She is humming to "ease the tension in the room."

As you see, the story Celina came up with has a simple sense of reality. I am saying that the things her characters say and do are necessary for them to say and do because of the circumstances they are living out and what it is they want to accomplish. And, these circumstances are something we can all believe would be possible within our own human sense of reality.

The next step for Celina would be to complete the nursery rhyme, in the manner she worked on in the first line, by using all the words of the nursery rhyme. Then, when she has completed creating her nursery rhyme play, Celina would work with some acting partners from class and put her play on its feet. Here's where Celina would get to be the director of her own nursery rhyme production. Also, when she begins to work with the other actors, with their help, Celina will quickly see where she needs to be more specific in defining the circumstances for each character so that everything that happens on stage is purposeful.

Larry: Celina, I know you haven't finished the whole nursery rhyme yet, but as a demonstration, I want you to work with your cast on what you have done so far. The rest of us will listen in on your work with the actors as you direct them. Is that okay?

Celina: Sure, that's fine.

Larry: Good. And I'll ask that you, and the actors working with you, be as specific as you can about everything you are doing. This will serve as a refresher on some things we have learned in class previously as well as figuring out how to put together this nursery rhyme project. Go ahead and begin, Celina.

Celina: Braeson, let's begin with you. You are playing the

Dad and I want you to stand at the door looking out to see if your fifteen-year-old daughter, Mary, is coming back for dinner. You are very upset with her.

Braeson: Why am I so upset with Mary?

Celina: That's a good question. I didn't figure that out specifically yet. Well... let's say that you have something important to tell the family tonight and you were planning to make your announcement at the dinner table because you want the whole family to hear. Yeah, that's good... let's say that you have some good news... no, you have great news!

Braeson: What's the great news?

Celina: Hmmm... How about you found out today that you got a promotion at work that will allow you to buy a new house for the family and you can get everyone out of this depressing dump you are all living in now.

Braeson: Hey, that's good. So, to begin, I will have to do an emotional preparation based on something incredibly wonderful that has happened to me.

Celina: Well... Braeson, remember that preparation is for the first moment only and then you don't know what will...

Braeson: Yeah, yeah, you're right. So, I have to make the wonderful thing specific and meaningful and then leave it alone. I have to know it and trust that when it needs to express itself, it will be there. Then, I have to prepare for how upset I am in the first moment. In this scene, I am upset about Mary not coming home on time, so for my preparation, I have to find something meaningful to me that will put me in that emotional state.

D'Vorah: May I chime in?

Celina: (*Laughs.*) Yes, my dear?

D'Vorah: (*Giggling back.*) I just wanted to say, since we are going over emotional preparation, that it is also important to drop the preparation once you come into the scene. I mean, we mustn't hold on to the preparation. We must leave it alone and allow ourselves to ride on the wave of "life" that the preparation has induced in us and then be willing to be fully available to our partners on stage and to work off of them in each moment.

Braeson: Yeah, I'm happy you said that, it's good to hear that again.

Celina: Okay, D'Vorah, as the Mom, the most important thing to you is that you keep things light and happy because you do not want to have this dinner end up in a big argument — which can happen when Dad is so upset. You are doing everything you can, as I wrote in the script, to ease the tension in the room. This includes your humming a happy tune, the way in which you serve the food to the family, and how you respond when the kids and Dad refuse to have the food you offer them.

D'Vorah: That's clear. Then the question I ask myself is,

why is it specifically important to me that there is no fighting at the table tonight?

Celina: Good, how would you like to set that up?

D'Vorah: Well, how about Sally came home from school very sad and crying because she and her best friend Gina had a big argument and are no longer best friends. Sally was sobbing and it took a long time for me to calm her down. Now, I don't like when there is fighting in the house at anytime and I especially don't want to have anything make Sally more upset tonight.

Celina: Great, I like that. And, that will help you, Meg, to play Sally. Your activity, Meg, while you are eating can be an internal one. Do you know what I mean?

Meg: Yes. How about I am trying to figure out what to say to Gina tomorrow at school so that we can be best friends again?

Celina: That will work nicely. Zach, you are playing Billy. You are making it very clear that you are displeased...

Zach: Yeah, that's why I turn down Mom's crummy food.

Celina: What might you be so displeased about?

Zach: Well, let's say that all my friends have new bikes and I am riding around on a real old beat-up one. I've been asking Dad for a new one for weeks and he just keeps saying, "We'll see."

Celina: Good. Even worse, the bike is Mary's old bike. It's a girl's bike that Dad put a makeshift bar on to make it look like a boy's bike. Now, what happened today that made this whole thing worse, specifically.

Zach: Uhmmm... I rode past this girl I have a crush on at school and she saw my bike and she and her girlfriend laughed at me.

Celina: So in your words and your behavior, you will show Mom and Dad that you are going to punish them until you get a new bike. Wow, you guys are great. This whole little scene really is starting to make sense now.

Larry: Yes, That's great. (*Larry addresses the whole class.*) Listen up everyone. I want you all to take a ten-minute break. Celina, please take your group into Studio Four and continue to work on your nursery rhyme. Everyone else, come back here after the break and, Miryame, we will work on your nursery rhyme next.

Celina: All right Larry. Come on everyone. (*Celina and her "cast" pick up their bags and stuff and head out of Studio Five. The other twenty students head out for their break. D'Vorah stops and comes back over to Larry.*)

D'Vorah: Larry, I had a kind of profound realization last night about this work. It's not really related to this new nursery rhyme exercise. It's more about everything we have been doing in class for the past six months. May I share it with you?

Larry: Yes. I am always up for a profound realization! (*They both laugh.*) May the readers listen in?

D'Vorah: Yes, I'd love for them to hear it too. What I realized is that the really big thing I am learning is that, after all the work is put in — you know, all the homework, and preparing, and fantasizing, and piecing together the puzzle of an exercise or a scene — that ultimately, we must be a vessel for some greater, I don't know, spirit, to speak through us. (*D'Vorah gets very quiet.*) That's the really big thing I am discovering here in class, that (*Tears now fall down D'Vorah's cheeks.*) I am a vessel. And that if I can really open up, something greater than me will come through me. And, when that happens, it's wonderful and it's joyous.

Larry: Yes, that's great D'Vorah. And you're right, that is profound. What you are speaking about is truly the sacred nature of our art.

D'Vorah: (*Taking a tissue out of her pocket, blowing her nose.*) Yes. Well, I just wanted to share that.

Larry: Thank you.

D'Vorah: Your welcome. I'm going to go join Celina and the gang. (*D'Vorah leaves Studio Five. Larry turns back to you, the readers.*)

Larry: All right, ready for your assignment? Here it is:

1. Find a nursery rhyme you would like to work on.

2. Out of your imagination, create a "play" that has

nothing to do with the characters or the circumstances of the original nursery rhyme.

3. Use every word of the nursery rhyme in the exact order. Do not add or change any words.

4. Make sure everything the characters do and say is justified, purposeful.

5. Your nursery rhyme play must be believable within a simple and human sense of reality. (For example, your scenario may include a dog and you may have an actor play the part of "the dog." But you wouldn't have the dog say any of the words of the nursery rhyme because, unlike *The Jetsons*, in our reality, dogs do not speak words. Although, the dog could certainly bark if it is justified.)

6. Once you have worked out your nursery rhyme play as best you can on your own, work with a group of acting partners and put your play "on it's feet." As Celina did with her actors, keep refining the play by asking the actors to help you get more and more specific in terms of "what" each character is doing and "why." Keep at it until you believe you have taken your play as far as you can in terms of justifying everything the characters say and do on stage.

7. One more thing. Although I have asked you to use a nursery rhyme for the purposes of this exercise, you may find other short pieces of text that are fun to use. For instance, when I was assigned this exercise at the Neighborhood Playhouse, I used an old story as my text. Here's how I set it up:

The circumstances I created were that my wife and I and our children were prisoners in a concentration camp. My wife and I had been ordered to come into the office of the commander who was going to tell us that either my wife or myself would be released from the camp with our children and that the other one of us would remain to face certain death.

I had four acting partners help me do my little play. One actor played the commander, and I directed him to have papers in front of him on a desk that listed prisoners who were being released from the camp. I also told him that when my wife and I sat down in front of him, he was to read the papers to himself and then simply point at me, which would inform the guards that I was going to be the one to leave with the children and that my wife was to be escorted back into the camp. I told the other two actors to be the guards and that once the decision had been made, one guard would take my wife out and the other guard would take me out. The other acting partner was my friend Loren, and she was going to play my wife. I told her that we were prisoners in a concentration camp with our children, and that we were just informed that one of us was going to be released from the camp with the children. I also told her that we were about to go in to see the commander and that he would point at the one of us who would be leaving with the children, and that the one of us not chosen would stay to die in the camp.

In doing it, I remember Loren and I sitting outside the room preparing together, and when we were both fully prepared, we held each other tightly and entered the room trembling, walking past the two guards who stood on each side of the door. We walked to two chairs in front of the desk of the commander and sat down, waiting while he read his papers silently. Finally, he looked up from his papers toward the guards and simply pointed at me, meaning that I was going to be taken out of the camp with the children and that my wife was to stay and die. Loren and I clutched each other tightly. We cried together and as we wept, I screamed out (the only line in my "nursery rhyme exercise"), pleading with the commander to, *"Take my wife...Please!"* Then the guards pulled us apart and escorted us out of the room.

So, for my exercise, I took the line, "Take my wife, please" and justified those words in a way that had nothing to do with the meaning of the joke.

Here are a few nursery rhymes for you. You may use any of these or you may want to look through some Mother Goose books for more options. (Or, as I did, you may find some other short piece of text to work with.)

I see the moon,
and the moon sees me;
God bless the moon,
And God bless me.

Little Tom Tucker
Sings for his supper;
What shall he eat?
White bread and butter.
How shall he cut it
Without e'er a knife?
How will he be married
Without e'er a wife?

Lucy Locket lost her pocket,
Kitty Fisher found it;
But ne'er a penny was there in it,
Except the binding round it.

Deedle, deedle, dumpling, my son John,
Went to bed with his breeches on;
One shoe off, and one shoe on,
Deedle, deedle, dumpling, my son John.

A swarm of bees in May
Is worth a load of hay;
A swarm of bees in June
Is worth a silver spoon;
A swarm of bees in July
Is not worth a fly.

Come, butter, come; come, butter, come.
Peter stands at the gate
Waiting for his buttered cake;
Come, butter, come.

Sing, sing! What shall I sing?
The cat's run away with the pudding bag string!

Cross Patch,
Draw the latch,
Sit by the fire and spin;
Take a cup,
And drink it up,
And call your neighbors in.

I had a little nut tree, nothing would it bear
But a silver nutmeg and a golden pear;
The king of Spain's daughter came to visit me,
And all for the sake of my little nut tree.
I skipped over the water, I danced over the sea,
And all the birds in the air couldn't catch me.

Pussy-Cat, Pussy-Cat,
Where have you been?
I've been to London
To visit the Queen.
Pussy-Cat, Pussy-Cat,
What did you there?
I frightened a little mouse
Under a chair.

All right, now I want you to get to work on your own nursery rhyme exercise.

The Original Nursery Rhyme:

_____

_____

_____

_____

_____

_____

_____

_____

_____

_____

The Characters in My Nursery Rhyme Play:

_____

_____

_____

_____

_____

_____

_____

The Circumstances of My Nursery Rhyme Play:

_____

_____

_____

_____

_____

_____

_____

My Play in Script Form:

_____

_____

_____

_____

_____

_____

_____

_____

_____

_____

_____

*The soul is made for action, and cannot rest
till it be employed. Idleness is its rust. Unless it will up
and think and taste and see, all is in vain.*
Thomas Traherne

chapter two

the scene

Here is a scene I will refer to later in the book. If you remember back to my Meisner Book Three, this scene from Horton Foote's beautiful play *A Young Lady of Property* appeared as the "Bonus Scene." Now, we will have the opportunity to look at the play in depth. Also, because we will be working on acting exercises in the context of the whole play, I have also included the entire play, *A Young Lady of Property,* here in the book for you.

I must stop a moment to thank my dear friend Horton for allowing me to use the play in this manner and for the continual inspiration he is in my life. If you haven't taken my advice yet, I will tell you again — get your hands on Horton's plays: any of them, all of them! You will be swept away by the richest, most soul-filled, and most deeply human of all modern American dramatic literature.

By the way, for our purposes here in Book Four, I am not requiring that you actually put the scene on its feet with an acting partner. (Although, if you are a young woman and would like to work on it with an acting partner, that would certainly be fine with me and you will have a real treat doing so.) My chief aim here is to give all of you a blueprint, a way of working with plays and with the characters in those plays *as an actor.* To do so, I will give you many exercises to complete as we concentrate on the character, Wilma.

You know, anyone can read a play and tell you the basic story line and circumstances. But your job will be to breathe life into those words on the page, which means that you have to become deeply sensitized to the text in ways that non-actors simply aren't. You must be able to investigate the play in ways that, ultimately, bring you and the "character" into very close contact.

First things first. Take some time right now and quietly read the scene:

(*Wilma sits in the swing rocking back and forth. ARABELLA comes running in r. c. of the yard area.*)

WILMA. Heh, Arabella. Come sit and swing.

ARABELLA. All right. Your letter came.

WILMA. Whoopee. Where is it?

ARABELLA. Here. (*She gives it to her. WILMA tears it open. She reads:*)

WILMA. "Dear Miss Thompson: Mr. Delafonte will be glad to see you anytime next week about your contemplated screen test. We suggest you call the office when you arrive in the city and we will set an exact time. Yours truly, Adele Murray." Well... Did you get yours?

ARABELLA. Yes.

WILMA. What did it say?

ARABELLA. The same.

WILMA. Exactly the same?

ARABELLA. Yes.

WILMA. Well, let's pack our bags. Hollywood, here we come.

ARABELLA. Wilma...

WILMA. Yes?

ARABELLA. I have to tell you something... Well... I...

WILMA. What is it?

ARABELLA. Well... promise me you won't hate me, or stop being my friend. I never had a friend, Wilma, until you began being nice to me, and I couldn't stand it if you weren't my friend any longer...

WILMA. Oh, my cow. Stop talking like that. I'll never stop being your friend. What do you want to tell me?

ARABELLA. Well... I don't want to go to see Mr. Delafonte, Wilma...

WILMA. You don't?

ARABELLA. No, I don't want to be a movie star. I don't want to leave Harrison or my mother or father... I just want to stay here the rest of my life and get married and settle down and have children.

WILMA. Arabella...

ARABELLA. I just pretended like I wanted to go to Hollywood because I knew you wanted me to, and I wanted you to like me...

WILMA. Oh, Arabella...

ARABELLA. Don't hate me, Wilma. You see, I'd be afraid... I'd die if I had to go to see Mr. Delafonte. Why, I even get faint when I have to recite before the class. I'm not like you. You're not scared of anything.

WILMA. Why do you say that?

ARABELLA. Because you're not. I know.

WILMA. Oh, yes, I am. I'm scared of lots of things.

ARABELLA. What.

WILMA. Getting lost in a city. Being bitten by dogs. Old lady Leighton taking my daddy away... (*A pause.*)

ARABELLA. Will you still be my friend?

WILMA. Sure. I'll always be your friend.

ARABELLA. I'm glad. Oh, I almost forgot. Your Aunt Gert said for you to come on home.

WILMA. I'll go in a little. I love to swing in my front yard. Aunt Gert has a swing in her front yard, but it's not the same. Mama and I used to come out here and swing together. Some nights when Daddy was out all night gambling, I used to wake up and hear her out here swinging away. Sometimes she'd let me come and sit beside her. We'd swing until three or four in the morning. (*A pause. She looks out into the yard.*) The pear tree looks sickly, doesn't it? The fig trees are doing nicely though. I was out in the back and the weeds are near knee high, but fig trees just seem to thrive in the weeds. The freeze must have killed off the banana trees... (*A pause. WILMA stops swinging – she walks around the yard.*) Maybe I won't leave either. Maybe I won't go to Hollywood after all.

ARABELLA. You won't?

WILMA. No. Maybe I shouldn't. That just comes to me now. You know sometimes my old house looks so lonesome it tears at my heart. I used to think it looked lonesome just whenever it had no tenants, but now it comes to me it has looked lonesome ever since Mama died and we moved away, and it will look lonesome until some of us move back here. Of course, Mama can't, and Daddy won't. So it's up to me.

ARABELLA. Are you gonna live here all by yourself?

WILMA. No. I talk big about living here by myself, but I'm too much of a coward to do that. But maybe I'll finish school and live with Aunt Gert and keep on renting the house until I meet some nice boy with good habits and steady ways, and marry him. Then we'll move here and have children and I bet this old house won't be lonely anymore. I'll get Mama's old croquet set and put it out under the pecan trees and play croquet with my children, or sit in this yard and swing and wave to people as they pass by.

ARABELLA. Oh, I wish you would. Mama says that's a normal life for a girl, marrying and having children. She says being an actress is all right, but the other's better.

WILMA. Maybe I've come to agree with your mama. Maybe I was going to Hollywood out of pure lonesomeness. I felt so alone with Mrs. Leighton getting my daddy and my mama having left the world. Daddy could have taken away my lonesomeness, but he didn't want to or couldn't. Aunt Gert says nobody is lonesome with a house full of children, so maybe that's what I just ought to stay here and have...

ARABELLA. Have you decided on a husband yet?

WILMA. No.

ARABELLA. Mama says that's the bad feature of being a girl, you have to wait for the boy to ask you and just pray that the one you want wants you. Tommy Murray is nice, isn't he?

WILMA. I think so.

ARABELLA. Jay Godfrey told me once he wanted to ask you for a date, but he didn't dare because he was afraid you'd turn him down.

WILMA. Why did he think that?

ARABELLA. He said the way you talked he didn't think you would go out with anything less than a movie star.

WILMA. Maybe you'd tell him different...

ARABELLA. All right. I think Jay Godfrey is very nice. Don't you?

WILMA. Yes, I think he's very nice and Tommy is nice...

ARABELLA. Maybe we could double-date sometimes.

WILMA. That might be fun.

ARABELLA. Oh, Wilma. Don't go to Hollywood. Stay here in Harrison and let's be friends forever...

WILMA. All right. I will.

ARABELLA. You will?

WILMA. Sure, why not? I'll stay here. I'll stay and marry and live in my house.

ARABELLA. Oh, Wilma. I'm so glad. I'm so very glad.

The first glance at History convinces us that the actions of men proceed from their needs, their passions, their characters and talents; and impresses us with the belief that such needs, passions and interests are the sole spring of actions.

Georg Hegel

chapter three

the play

Now that you have read the scene, I want you to read the entire play. Again, find a quiet place where you will not be disturbed and simply read the play. As best you can, do not try to make any decisions about anything as you read. See if you can allow the words to work on you in their own mysterious way.

After you read the play, I want you to immediately complete the writing assignment that I will give to you at the end of the script. So make sure you have enough time to both read the play and to do some writing. If you are ready, Go ahead now and read the play.

A Young Lady of Property by Horton Foote
Cast: Miss Martha Davenport
            Mr. Russell Walter Graham

Wilma Thompson
Arabella Cookenboo
Lester Thompson
Mrs. Leighton
Minna Boyd
Miss Gert
Man

Place: Harrison, Texas
Time: Late Spring, 1925

The stage is divided into four areas. Area one, directly across the front of the stage is a sidewalk. Area two, just above the sidewalk L. of C., is a part of a kitchen. A table, with a portable phonograph on it, and four chairs are placed here. Area three is above the sidewalk R. of C. It has a yard swing in it. Area four is directly U. C. In it is a post office window.

The lights are brought up on the post office window. It is attended by two people, MISS MARTHA DAVENPORT, who is inside the window, and MR. RUSSELL WALTER GRAHAM, who is leaning on the outside ledge of the window. It is about three-thirty of a late spring day. MISS MARTHA and MR. RUSSELL WALTER look very sleepy. Two girls around fifteen come in with schoolbooks in their arms. They are WILMA THOMPSON and ARABELLA COOKENBOO. WILMA is a handsome girl with style and spirit about her. ARABELLA is gentle looking, so shy about growing into womanhood that one can't really tell yet what she is to look like or become. She is WILMA'S shadow and obviously her adoring slave. They go up to the window. MR. RUSSELL WALTER sees them and punches MISS MARTHA.

RUSSELL. Look who's here, Miss Martha. The Bobbsey twins.

(MISS MARTHA gives a peal of laughter that sounds as if she thought MR. RUSSELL WALTER the funniest man in the five counties.)

MISS MARTHA. *(Again giggling.)* Now, Mr. Russell Walter, don't start teasing the young ladies. How are you girls?

WILMA and ARABELLA. Fine.

RUSSELL. Can I sell you any stamps? We have some lovely special deliveries today. Our one's and two's are very nice too.

MARTHA. *(Giggling.)* Isn't he a tease, girls?

WILMA. Mr. Russell Walter, when's the next train in from Houston?

RUSSELL. Why? Going on a trip?

MARTHA. *(Rolling at his wit.)* Now, Mr. Russell Walter, stop teasing the young ladies. The next mail doesn't come in on the train, dear ones, it comes in on the bus. And that will be at six. Although the Houston mail is usually very light at that time, there are a few special deliveries. Do you think your letter might come by special delivery, Wilma?

WILMA. No ma'm. Regular.

MARTHA. Oh. Well, in that case I don't hold out much

hope for it on that delivery. It's usually mostly second-class mail. You know, seed catalogues and such. The next Houston mail heavy with first-class is delivered at five tomorrow morning.

RUSSELL. Which she knows better than you.

MARTHA. (*Giggling.*) Now, Mr. Russell Walter, stop teasing the young ladies.

WILMA. Arabella and I were discussing coming here from school, Mr. Russell Walter, that the mail sometimes gets in the wrong box.

RUSSELL. Rarely, Miss Wilma. Rarely.

WILMA. Arabella says that once a Christmas card meant for her got put by mistake in Box 270, instead of her box which is 370, and she didn't get it back until the third of January.

RUSSELL. Well, if that happens, nothing we can do about it until the person whose box it got into by mistake returns it.

WILMA. Yes sir. (*A pause.*) I don't suppose any mail has been put in my box since my Aunt Gert was here last.

RUSSELL. Well, seeing as she was here just a half hour ago, I don't think so.

MARTHA. Who are you expecting a letter from, young lady?

WILMA. Somebody very important. Come on, Arabella. (*They start out. They pause. She goes back to the window.*) Mr. Russell Walter, once I had a movie star picture, Ben Lyons I think, that was addressed to Wilma Thomas instead of Thompson, and if you remember, Mr. Peter was new at the time and put it into General Delivery, and it wasn't until two weeks later that you discovered it there and figured it belonged to me.

RUSSELL. Well, Mr. Peter isn't new here now.

WILMA. But I thought maybe accidentally someone put my letter in General Delivery.

RUSSELL. Nope.

MARTHA. Oh, Mr. Walter. Go ahead and look. It won't hurt you.

RUSSELL. Now, Miss Martha...

MARTHA. Now just go ahead... (*She hands him a stack of letters.*)

RUSSELL. All right... Anything to please the ladies. (*He goes over the letters and starts looking into them.*)

MARTHA. Wilma, I saw your daddy and Mrs. Leighton at the picture show together again last night. Maybe you'll be having a new mother soon.

WILMA. Well, I wouldn't hold my breath waiting if I were you.

MARTHA. I was saying to Mr. Russell Walter I see the tenants have left the Thompson house. Maybe they were asked to leave so Mr. Thompson might move in with a bride.

WILMA. They were asked to leave because they were tearing it to pieces. They had weeds growing in the yards and had torn off wallpaper. My aunt Gert asked them to leave...

MARTHA. Oh, of course. They didn't take any pride in it at all. Not like when your mother was living. Why, I remember your mother always had the yard filled with flowers, and... (*The phone rings.*) Excuse me. (*MISS MARTHA answers it.*) Post office. Yes. Yes. She's here. Yes, I will. (*She puts the phone down.*) That was your Aunt Gertrude, Wilma. She said you were to come right home.

WILMA. All right.

MARTHA. Found any mail for Wilma, Mr. Russell Walter?

RUSSELL. Nope, Miss Wilma. No mail, and no female either.

MARTHA. (*Giggling.*) Isn't he a sight? You come back at six, Wilma. Maybe we'll have something then.

WILMA. Yes ma'am. Come on, Arabella.

(*They go outside the area and walk directly down the c. of the stage and pause at the apron looking up and down. They are now on the sidewalk area.*)

WILMA. I'd like to scratch that old cat's eyes out. The idea of her saying old lady Leighton is going to be my mother. She's so nosy. I wonder how she'd like it if I asked her if Mr. Russell Walter was going to ask her to marry him after she's been chasing him for fifteen years.

ARABELLA. Well, just ignore her.

WILMA. I intend to.

ARABELLA. What are you going to do now, Wilma?

WILMA. Fool around until the six o'clock mail.

ARABELLA. Don't you think you ought to go home like your aunt said?

WILMA. No.

ARABELLA. Have you told your Aunt Gert about the letter you're expecting yet?

WILMA. No.

ARABELLA. When are you going to tell her?

WILMA. Not until it comes. I think I'll go over and see my house. Look at how those tenants left it. I may have to sell it yet to get me to Hollywood...

ARABELLA. Wilma, is that house really yours?

WILMA. Sure it's mine. My mother left it to me.

ARABELLA. Well, do you get the rent for it and tell them who to rent to like Papa does his rent houses?

WILMA. No. But it's understood it's mine. My mother told Aunt Gert it was mine just before she died. Daddy had put it in her name because he was gambling terrible then, and Aunt Gert says Mama was afraid they'd lose it. I let Daddy rent it and keep the money now. Aunt Gert says I should as he is having a very hard time. His job at the cotton gin doesn't pay hardly anything. Of course, I feel very lucky having my own house.

ARABELLA. Well, I have a house.

WILMA. Do you own it yourself?

ARABELLA. No. But I live in it.

WILMA. Well, that's hardly the same thing. I own a house, which is very unusual, Aunt Gert says, for a girl of fifteen. I'm a young lady of property, Aunt Gert says. Many's the time I thought I'll just go and live in it all by myself. Wouldn't Harrison sit up and take notice then? Once when I was thirteen and I was very fond of my Cousin Neeley I thought I'd offer it to him to get through law school. But I'm glad I didn't since he turned out so hateful. (*A pause.*) Do you remember when I used to live in my house?

ARABELLA. No.

WILMA. Well, it's a long time ago now, but I still remember it. My mama and I used to play croquet in the yard under the pecan trees. We'd play croquet every afternoon just before sundown and every once in a while she'd stop the game and ask me to run to the corner without letting the neighbors know what I was doing, to see if my father was coming home. She always worried about his getting home by six, because if he wasn't there by then she knew it meant trouble. My mother always kept me in white starched dresses. Do you remember my mother?

ARABELLA. No. But my mother does. She says she was beautiful, with the disposition of a saint.

WILMA. I know. Her name was Alice. Isn't that a pretty name?

ARABELLA. Yes. It is.

WILMA. There's a song named "Sweet Alice Ben Bolt." Aunt Gert used to sing it all the time. When Mama died, she stopped. My mama died of a broken heart.

ARABELLA. She did?

WILMA. Oh, yes. Even Aunt Gert admits that. Daddy's gambling broke her heart. Oh, well. What are you gonna do about it? Boy, I used to hate my daddy. I used to dream about what I'd do to him when I grew up. But he's sorry now and reformed, so I've forgiven him.

ARABELLA. Oh, sure. You shouldn't hate your father.

WILMA. Well, I don't know. Do you know something I've never told another living soul?

ARABELLA. What?

WILMA. Swear you won't tell?

ARABELLA. I swear.

WILMA. I love him now. Sometimes I think I'd give up this whole movie star business if I could go back to our house and live with Daddy and keep house for him. But Aunt Gert says under the circumstances that's not practical. I guess you and everybody else knows what the circumstances are. Mrs. Leighton. She's got my Daddy hogtied. Aunt Gert says she isn't good enough to shine my mother's shoes, and I think she's right.

(*MISS MARTHA comes out of the post office area u. c. She walks halfway down the c. of the stage.*)

MARTHA. Are you girls still here?

WILMA. Yes ma'm.

MARTHA. Minna called this time, Wilma. She said you were to come home immediately. (*MISS MARTHA goes back inside the post office area and into her window u. c.*)

ARABELLA. Now come on, Wilma. You'll just get in trouble.

WILMA. All right. (*They start off r. WILMA stops. She looks panicky.*) Wait a minute, Arabella. Yonder comes my daddy walking with that fool Mrs. Leighton. I just as soon I didn't have to see them. Let's go the other way. (*They turn around and start l. A man's voice calls in* the distance: *"Wilma, Wilma." WILMA and ARABELLA stop. WILMA whispers:*) That's the kind of luck I have. He saw me. Now I'll have to speak to old lady Leighton.

ARABELLA. Don't you like her?

WILMA. Do you like snakes?

ARABELLA. No.

WILMA. Well, neither do I like Mrs. Leighton and for the same reason.

(*LESTER THOMPSON and MRS. LEIGHTON enter from d. r. LESTER is a handsome, weak man in his forties. MRS. LEIGHTON is thirty-five or so, blonde, pretty, and completely unlike WILMA'S description. There is a warmth about her that we should wish that WILMA might notice. LESTER goes over to WILMA.*)

LESTER. (*As he leaves MRS. LEIGHTON.*) Excuse me, Sibyl. Wilma...

WILMA. Yes sir.

LESTER. Say hello to Mrs. Leighton.

WILMA. (*Most ungraciously.*) Hello, Mrs. Leighton.

MRS. LEIGHTON. (*Most graciously.*) Hello, Wilma.

LESTER. What are you doing hanging around the streets, Wilma?

WILMA. Waiting to see if I have a letter.

LESTER. What kind of letter Wilma?

WILMA. About getting into the movies. Arabella and I saw an ad in the *Houston Chronicle* about a Mr. Delafonte who is a famous Hollywood director.

LESTER. Who is Mr. Delafonte?

WILMA. The Hollywood director I'm trying to tell you about. He's giving screen tests in Houston to people of beauty and talent, and if they pass they'll go to Hollywood and be in the picture shows.

LESTER. Well, that's all a lot of foolishness, Wilma. You're not going to Houston to take anything.

WILMA. But, Daddy... I...

LESTER. You're fifteen years old and you're gonna stay home like a fifteen-year-old girl should. There'll be plenty of time to go to Houston.

WILMA. But, Daddy, Mr. Delafonte won't be there forever.

LESTER. Go on home, Wilma.

WILMA. But Daddy...

LESTER. Don't argue with me. I want you to march home just as quick as you can, young lady. I'm going to stand right here until you turn that corner and if I ever catch you hanging around the streets again, it will be between you and me.

WILMA. Yes sir. Come on, Arabella.

(*She and ARABELLA walk out l. LESTER stands watching. SYBIL LEIGHTON comes up to him.*)

MRS. LEIGHTON. Have you told her we're getting married, Lester?

LESTER. No, I'm telling Gert tonight.

MRS. LEIGHTON. Aren't you going to tell Wilma?

LESTER. No. Gert's the one to tell her. Wilma and I have very little to say to each other. Gert has won her over completely.

MRS. LEIGHTON. They must be expecting it. Why would they think you're selling your house and quitting your job?

LESTER. I don't think they know that either. I'll explain the whole thing to Gert tonight. Come on. She's turned the corner. I think she'll go on home now.

(*They walk on and off. The lights are brought up d. l. in area 2. It is a part of the kitchen in GERTRUDE MILLER'S house. MINNA BOYD, a thin, strong Negro woman in her middle forties, is seated at the table. She has a portable hand-winding Victrola on the table. She is listening to a jazz recording. WILMA and ARABELLA come in u. c. of the kitchen area.*)

MINNA. Well, here's the duchess. Arrived at last. Where have you been, Wilma? What on earth do you mean aggravating us this way? Your Aunt Gert was almost late for her card party worrying over you.

WILMA. You knew where I was. You called often enough. I was at the post office waiting for the mail.

MINNA. How many times has Miss Gert told you not to hang around there? Where's your pride? You know Mr. Russell Walter called and told her you were about to drive them crazy down at the post office. He said when you got your letter he's gonna be so relieved he'll deliver it in person. Your aunt says you're to get right to your room and study.

WILMA. We're just going. Come on Arabella.

MINNA. And without Arabella. I know how much studying you and Arabella will do. You'll spend your whole time talking about Hollywood and picture shows. Clara Bow this and Alice White that. You go in there and learn something. The principal called your auntie this morning and told her you were failing in your typing and shorthand.

WILMA. (*Very bored.*) Well, I don't care. I hate them. I never wanted to take them anyway.

MINNA. Never mind about that. You just get in there and get to it. (*Wilma pays no attention. She goes deliberately and sits in a chair, scowling.*) Wilma...

WILMA. What?

MINNA. Now why do you want to act like this?

WILMA. Like what?

MINNA. So ugly. Your face is gonna freeze like that one day and then you're gonna be in a nice how-do-you-do.

ARABELLA. I'd better go, Wilma.

WILMA. All right, Arabella. Someday soon I'll be established in my own house and then you won't be treated so rudely.

MINNA. You come back some other time.

ARABELLA. Thank you, I will.

WILMA. I'll never get out of the house again today, Arabella, so will you check on the six o'clock mail?

ARABELLA. All right.

WILMA. Come right over if I have a letter.

ARABELLA. All right. Good-bye.

(*ARABELLA goes out u. c. of the kitchen area and goes offstage. WILMA plunks an imaginary guitar and sings, in an exaggerated hillbilly style,* "Write me a letter. Send it by mail. Send it in care of Birmingham jail.")

MINNA. Wilma, what is that letter about you're expectin'? Have you got a beau for yourself?

WILMA. Don't be crazy.

MINNA. Look at me.

WILMA. I said no, and stop acting crazy. I'm expecting a letter from Mr. Delafonte.

MINNA. Mr. Who?

WILMA. Mr. Delafonte, the famous movie director.

MINNA. Never heard of him.

WILMA. Well, I wouldn't let anyone know if I was that ignorant. The whole world has heard of Mr. Delafonte. He has only directed Pola Negri and Betty Compson and Lila Lee and I don't know who all.

MINNA. What are you hearing from Mr. Delafonte about?

WILMA. A Hollywood career.

MINNA. What are you going to do with a Hollywood career?

WILMA. Be a movie star, you goose. First he's going to screen-test me, and then I'll go to Hollywood and be a Wampus baby star.

MINNA. A what?

WILMA. A Wampus baby star. You know. That's what you are before you are a movie star. You get chosen to be a Wampus baby star and parade around in a bathing suit and get all your pictures in the papers and the movie magazines.

MINNA. I want to see Miss Gert's face when you start parading around in a bathing suit for magazines. And what's all this got to do with a letter?

WILMA. Well, I read in a Houston paper where Mr. Delafonte was in Houston interviewing people at his studio for Hollywood screen tests. So Arabella and I wrote him for an appointment.

MINNA. And that's what your letter is all about? No gold mine. No oil well. Just Mr. Delafonte and a movie test.

WILMA. Yes. And if you be nice to me, after I win the screen test and sell my house I might take you out with me.

MINNA. Sell your what?

WILMA. My house.

MINNA. Wilma... why don't you stop talking like that?...

WILMA. Well, it's my house. I can sell it if I want to.

MINNA. You can't.

WILMA. I can.

MINNA. That house wasn't given to you to sell. A fifteen-year-old child. Who do you think is gonna let you sell it?

WILMA. Haven't you told me the house was mine? Hasn't Aunt Gert?

MINNA. Yes, but not to sell and throw the money away. And besides, it looks like to me the house is gonna be having permanent visitors soon.

WILMA. Who?

MINNA. What you don't know won't hurt you.

WILMA. If you mean my daddy and old lady Leighton, I'd burn it down first.

MINNA. Wilma.

WILMA. I will, I'll burn it down right to the ground.

(*Miss Gert comes in d. l. of the kitchen area. She is in her forties, handsome and tall.*)

MINNA. Hello, Miss Gert...

GERT. Hello, Minna. Hello, Wilma.

MINNA. How was the party?

GERT. All right. Minna, Neely is going to be away tonight so don't fix any supper for him and we had refreshments at the party so I'm not hungry. (*She suddenly bursts out crying and has to leave the room. She goes running out d. l. of the kitchen area.*)

WILMA. Now what's the matter with her?

MINNA. Sick headache likely. You stay here, I'll go see.

WILMA. All right. If she wants any ice, I'll crack it.

> (*MINNA goes out d. l. of the kitchen area. WILMA turns on the phonograph and plays a popular song of the 1920s.*)

MINNA: (*Comes back in.*) We better turn that off. She's got a bad one. First sick headache she's had in three years. I remember the last one.

WILMA. Does she want any cracked ice?...

MINNA. No

WILMA. Did she hear any bad news?

MINNA. I don't know.

WILMA. Can I go in to see her?

MINNA. Nope. You can please her, though, by getting into your studying.

WILMA. If you won't let me sell my house and go to Hollywood, I'll just quit school and move over there and rent out rooms. Support myself that way.

MINNA. You won't do nothin' of the kind. You go in there now and study.

WILMA. Why do I have to study? I have a house... and...

MINNA. Wilma, will you stop talking crazy?

WILMA. I'm not talking crazy. I could think of worse things to do. I'll rent out rooms and sit on the front porch and rock and be a lady of mystery, like a lady I read about once that locked herself in her house. Let the vines grow all around. Higher and higher until all light was shut out. She was eighteen when the vines started growing, and when she died and they cut the vines down and found her she was seventy-three and in all that time she had never put her foot outside once. All her family and friends were dead...

MINNA. I know you're crazy now.

WILMA. Minna... Minna... (*She runs to her.*) I'm scared. I'm scared.

MINNA. What in the name of goodness are you scared of?

WILMA. I'm scared my daddy is going to marry Mrs. Leighton.

MINNA. Now... now... (*Holds her.*)

WILMA. Minna, let me run over to my house for just a little bit. I can't ever go over there when there's tenants living in it. I feel the need of seeing it. I'll come right back.

MINNA. Will you promise me to come right back?

WILMA. I will.

MINNA. And you'll get right to your studying and no more arguments?

WILMA. No more.

MINNA. All right, then run on.

WILMA. Oh, Minna. I love you. And you know what I'm going to do? I'm going to be a great movie star and send my chauffeur and my limousine to Harrison and put you in it and drive you all the way to Hollywood.

MINNA. Thank you.

WILMA. H.O.B.

MINNA. H.O.B.? What's H.O.B.?

WILMA. Hollywood or bust!... (*She goes running out u. c. of the kitchen area. MINNA calls after her:*)

MINNA. Don't forget to get right back.

(*We hear WILMA'S voice answering in the distance: "All right." The lights are brought down. The lights are brought immediately up in the kitchen, a half-hour later. AUNT GERT comes in d. l. of the area. She has on a dressing gown. Twilight is beginning. She switches on a light. She looks around the room. She calls:*)

GERT. Minna, Minna. (*A pause. She calls again:*) Minna. Minna.

(*In comes ARABELLA u. c. of the area. She is carrying two letters:*)

ARABELLA. Hello, Miss Gertrude.

GERT. Hello Arabella.

ARABELLA. Where's Wilma?

GERT. I don't know. The door to her room was closed
when I went by. I guess she's in there studying.

ARABELLA. Yes'm. (*She starts out of the room d. l. of the
area.*)

GERT. Arabella.

(*ARABELLA pauses.*)

ARABELLA. Yes'm.

GERT. Wilma's gotten behind in her schoolwork, so please
don't ask her to go out anyplace tonight, because I'll
have to say no, and...

ARABELLA. Oh, no ma'm. I just brought her letter over to
her. She asked me to get it if it came in on the six
o'clock mail and it did.

GERT. Is that the letter she's been driving us all crazy
about?

ARABELLA. Yes ma'm, I got one too. (*She holds two letters
up. Puts one on the table.*)

GERT. Oh. Well... (*ARABELLA starts out again d. l. of the
area.*) Arabella, what is in that letter?

ARABELLA. Hasn't Wilma told you yet?

GERT. No.

ARABELLA. Then you'd better find out from her. She might be mad if I told you.

GERT. All right. (*ARABELLA starts out of the room.*) You didn't see Minna out in the backyard as you were coming in, did you?

ARABELLA. No.

GERT. I wonder where she can be. It's six-fifteen and she hasn't started a thing for supper yet.

(*ARABELLA goes out d. l. of the area and looks out an imaginary window r. c. She comes back in the room.*)

ARABELLA. Wilma isn't in the bedroom.

GERT. She isn't?

ARABELLA. No ma'm. Not in the front room either. I went in there.

GERT. That's strange. Isn't that strange? (*MINNA comes in u. c. of the area. She has a package in her hand.*) Oh, there you are, Minna.

MINNA. I had to run to the store for some baking soda. How do you feel? (*MINNA puts the package on the table.*)

GERT. Better. Where's Wilma?

MINNA. You don't mean she's not back yet?

GERT. Back? Where did she go?

MINNA. She swore to me if I let her go over to her house for a few minutes she'd be back here and study with no arguments.

GERT. Well, she's not here.

MINNA. That's the trouble with her. Give her an inch and she'll take a mile.

GERT. Arabella, would you run over to Wilma's house and tell her to get right home?

ARABELLA. Yes ma'm.

(She picks the letter up off the table and takes it with her as she goes out d. l. of the area. A knock is heard offstage.)

GERT. (*Calling.*) Come in. (*MISS MARTHA comes in u. c. of the area.*) Oh, hello, Miss Martha.

MARTHA. Hello, Gert. Hello, Minna.

MINNA. Hello, Miss Martha...

MARTHA. I thought you'd be back here. I knocked and knocked at your front door and no one answered, but I knew somebody must be here this time of day, so I just decided to come on back.

GERT. I'm glad you did. We can't hear a knock at the front door back here. Sit down, won't you?

MARTHA. I can't stay a second. I just wanted to tell Wilma that her letter arrived on the six o'clock bus.

GERT. She knows, thank you, Miss Martha. Arabella brought it over to her.

MARTHA. Oh, the address on the back said the Delafonte Studio. I wonder what that could be?

GERT. I don't know.

MINNA. I knows. It's the moving pictures. She wrote about getting into them.

GERT. I do declare. She's always up to something.

MARTHA. Well, I never heard of moving pictures in Houston. I just heard the news about Lester. Was I surprised! Were you?

GERT. Yes, I was.

MARTHA. When's the wedding taking place?

GERT. I don't know.

MARTHA. Oh, I see. Well, I have to run on now.

GERT. All right, thank you, Miss Martha, for coming by. I know Wilma will appreciate it.

MARTHA. I'll just go out the back way if you don't mind. It'll save me a few steps.

GERT. Of course not.

MARTHA. Good night.

GERT. Good night, Miss Martha. (*She goes out u. c. of the area.*)

MINNA. What news is this?

GERT. Oh, you must know, Minna. Lester and Mrs. Leighton are getting married at last. That's why I came home from the party all upset. I had to hear about my own brother's marriage at a bridge party. And I know it's true. It came straight from the county clerk's office. They got their license this morning.

MINNA. Well, poor Wilma. She'll take this hard.

GERT. She's going to take it very hard. But what can you do? What can you do?

(*They both sit dejectedly at the table. The lights fade in the area d. l. as they come up on the area d. r. WILMA comes in from u. c. of the d. r. area. It is the yard of her house. She sits in the swing rocking back and forth, singing "Birmingham Jail" in her hillbilly style. ARABELLA comes running in r. c. of the yard area.*)

WILMA. Heh, Arabella. Come sit and swing.

ARABELLA. All right. Your letter came.

WILMA. Whoopee. Where is it?

ARABELLA. Here. (*She gives it to her. WILMA tears it open. She reads:*)

WILMA. "Dear Miss Thompson: Mr. Delafonte will be glad to see you anytime next week about your contemplated screen test. We suggest you call the office when you arrive in the city and we will set an exact time. Yours truly, Adele Murray." Well... Did you get yours?

ARABELLA. Yes.

WILMA. What did it say?

ARABELLA. The same.

WILMA. Exactly the same?

ARABELLA. Yes.

WILMA. Well, let's pack our bags. Hollywood, here we come.

ARABELLA. Wilma...

WILMA. Yes?

ARABELLA. I have to tell you something... Well... I...

WILMA. What is it?

ARABELLA. Well... promise me you won't hate me, or stop being my friend. I never had a friend, Wilma, until you began being nice to me, and I couldn't stand it if you weren't my friend any longer...

WILMA. Oh, my cow. Stop talking like that. I'll never stop being your friend. What do you want to tell me?

ARABELLA. Well... I don't want to go to see Mr. Delafonte, Wilma...

WILMA. You don't?

ARABELLA. No, I don't want to be a movie star. I don't want to leave Harrison or my mother or father... I just want to stay here the rest of my life and get married and settle down and have children.

WILMA. Arabella...

ARABELLA. I just pretended like I wanted to go to Hollywood because I knew you wanted me to, and I wanted you to like me...

WILMA. Oh, Arabella...

ARABELLA. Don't hate me, Wilma. You see, I'd be afraid... I'd die if I had to go to see Mr. Delafonte. Why, I even get faint when I have to recite before the class. I'm not like you. You're not scared of anything.

WILMA. Why do you say that?

ARABELLA. Because you're not. I know.

WILMA. Oh, yes, I am. I'm scared of lots of things.

ARABELLA. What.

WILMA. Getting lost in a city. Being bitten by dogs. Old lady Leighton taking my daddy away... (*A pause.*)

ARABELLA. Will you still be my friend?

WILMA. Sure. I'll always be your friend.

ARABELLA. I'm glad. Oh, I almost forgot. Your Aunt Gert said for you to come on home.

WILMA. I'll go in a little. I love to swing in my front yard. Aunt Gert has a swing in her front yard, but it's not the same. Mama and I used to come out here and swing together. Some nights when Daddy was out all night gambling, I used to wake up and hear her out here swinging away. Sometimes she'd let me come and sit beside her. We'd swing until three or four in the morning. (*A pause. She looks out into the yard.*) The pear tree looks sickly, doesn't it? The fig trees are doing nicely though. I was out in the back and the weeds are near knee high, but fig trees just seem to thrive in the weeds. The freeze must have killed off the banana trees... (*A pause. WILMA stops swinging — she walks around the yard.*) Maybe I won't leave either. Maybe I won't go to Hollywood after all.

ARABELLA. You won't?

WILMA. No. Maybe I shouldn't. That just comes to me now. You know sometimes my old house looks so lonesome it tears at my heart. I used to think it looked lonesome just whenever it had no tenants, but now it comes to me it has looked lonesome ever since Mama died and we moved away, and it will look lonesome until some of us move back here. Of course, Mama can't, and Daddy won't. So it's up to me.

ARABELLA. Are you gonna live here all by yourself?

WILMA. No. I talk big about living here by myself, but I'm too much of a coward to do that. But maybe I'll finish school and live with Aunt Gert and keep on renting the house until I meet some nice boy with good habits and steady ways, and marry him. Then we'll move here and have children and I bet this old house won't be lonely anymore. I'll get Mama's old croquet set and put it out under the pecan trees and play croquet with my children, or sit in this yard and swing and wave to people as they pass by.

ARABELLA. Oh, I wish you would. Mama says that's a normal life for a girl, marrying and having children. She says being an actress is all right, but the other's better.

WILMA. Maybe I've come to agree with your mama. Maybe I was going to Hollywood out of pure lonesomeness. I felt so alone with Mrs. Leighton getting my daddy and my mama having left the world. Daddy could have taken away my lonesomeness, but he didn't want to or couldn't. Aunt Gert says nobody is lonesome with a house full of children, so maybe that's what I just ought to stay here and have...

ARABELLA. Have you decided on a husband yet?

WILMA. No.

ARABELLA. Mama says that's the bad feature of being a girl, you have to wait for the boy to ask you and just pray that the one you want wants you. Tommy Murray is nice, isn't he?

WILMA. I think so.

ARABELLA. Jay Godfrey told me once he wanted to ask you for a date, but he didn't dare because he was afraid you'd turn him down.

WILMA. Why did he think that?

ARABELLA. He said the way you talked he didn't think you would go out with anything less than a movie star.

WILMA. Maybe you'd tell him different...

ARABELLA. All right. I think Jay Godfrey is very nice. Don't you?

WILMA. Yes, I think he's very nice and Tommy is nice...

ARABELLA. Maybe we could double-date sometimes.

WILMA. That might be fun.

ARABELLA. Oh, Wilma. Don't go to Hollywood. Stay here in Harrison and let's be friends forever...

WILMA. All right. I will.

ARABELLA. You will?

WILMA. Sure, why not? I'll stay here. I'll stay and marry and live in my house.

ARABELLA. Oh, Wilma. I'm so glad. I'm so very glad.

(*WILMA gets back in the swing. They swing vigorously back and forth... A MAN comes in r. c. of the yard area.*)

MAN. I beg your pardon. Is this the Thompson house?

(*They stop swinging.*)

WILMA. Yes sir.

MAN. I understand it's for sale. I'd like to look around.

WILMA. No sir. It's not for sale. It's for rent. I'm Wilma Thompson. I own the house. My daddy rents it for me...

MAN. Oh, well, we were told by Mr. Mavis...

WILMA. I'm sure. Mr. Mavis tries to sell everything around here. He's pulled that once before about our house, but this house is not for sale. It's for rent.

MAN. You're sure?

WILMA. I'm positive. We rent it for twenty-seven fifty a month. You pay lights, water, and keep the yard clean. We are very particular over how the yard is kept. I'd be glad to show it to you...

MAN. I'm sorry. I was interested in buying. There must have been a mistake.

WILMA. There must have been.

MAN. Where could I find your father, young lady?

WILMA. Why do you want to see him?

MAN. Well, I'd just like to get this straight. I understood from Mr. Mavis...

WILMA. Mr. Mavis has nothing to do with my house. My house is for rent, not for sale.

MAN. All right. (*The MAN leaves. He goes out r. c. of the yard area.*)

WILMA. The nerve of old man Mavis putting out around town that my house is for sale. Isn't that nervy, Arabella?

(*ARABELLA gets out of the swing.*)

ARABELLA. We'd better go. It'll be dark soon. The tree frogs are starting.

WILMA. It just makes me furious. Wouldn't it make you furious?

ARABELLA. Come on. Let's go.

WILMA. Wouldn't it make you furious?

ARABELLA. Yes.

WILMA. You don't sound like you mean it.

ARABELLA. Well...

WILMA. Well... What?...

ARABELLA. Nothing... Let's go.

WILMA. Arabella, you know something you're not telling me.

ARABELLA. No, I don't. Honest, Wilma...

WILMA. You do. Look at me, Arabella...

ARABELLA. I don't know anything. I swear...

WILMA. You do. I thought you were my friend.

ARABELLA. I am. I am.

WILMA. Well, then why don't you tell me?

ARABELLA. Because I promised not to.

WILMA. Why?

ARABELLA. Well... I...

WILMA. What is it? Arabella, please tell me.

ARABELLA. Well... Will you never say I told you?

WILMA. I swear.

ARABELLA. Well, I didn't tell you before because in all the excitement in telling you I wasn't going to Hollywood and your saying you weren't going, I forgot about it... until that man came...

WILMA. What is it, Arabella? What is it?

ARABELLA. Well, I heard my daddy tell my mother that Mr. Lester had taken out a license to marry Mrs. Leighton.

WILMA. Oh, well. That doesn't surprise me too much. I've been looking for that to happen.

ARABELLA. But that isn't all, Wilma...

WILMA. What else?

ARABELLA. Well...

WILMA. What else?

ARABELLA. Well...

WILMA. What else, Arabella? What else?...

ARABELLA. Well... My daddy heard that your daddy had put this house up for sale...

WILMA. I don't believe you...

ARABELLA. That's what he said, Wilma... I... He said Mr.

Lester came to him and wanted to know if he wanted to buy it...

WILMA. Well. He won't do it. Not my house. He won't do it! (*WILMA has jumped out of the swing and runs out of the yard u. c.*)

ARABELLA. Wilma... Wilma... Please... don't say I said it... Wilma...

(*She is standing alone and frightened as the lights fade. The lights are brought up in the area l. of c. MINNA is mixing some dough on the table. MISS GERT comes in.*)

GERT. She's not back yet?

MINNA. No. I knew when Arabella took that letter over there she wouldn't be here until good dark.

GERT. I just put in a call for Lester... He is going to have to tell her about the marriage. It's his place. Don't you think so?

MINNA. I certainly do. I most certainly do.

(*WILMA comes running in u. c. of the kitchen area.*)

WILMA. Aunt Gert, do you know where I can find my daddy?

GERT. No, Wilma... I...

WILMA. Well, I've got to find him. I went over to the cotton gin but he'd left. I called out to his boardinghouse and he wasn't there...

GERT. Well, I don't know, Wilma...

WILMA. Is he gonna sell my house?

GERT. Wilma...

WILMA. Is he or isn't he?

GERT. I don't know anything about it...

WILMA. Well, something's going on. Let me tell you that. I was sitting in the swing with Arabella when a man came up and said he wanted to buy it, and I said to rent and he said to buy, that Mr. Mavis had sent him over, and I told him he was mistaken and he left. Well, I was plenty mad at Mr. Mavis and told Arabella so, but she looked funny and I got suspicious and I finally got it out of her that Daddy was going to marry old lady Leighton and was putting my house up for sale... (*Gert is crying.*) Aunt Gert. Isn't that my house?

GERT. Yes. I'd always thought so...

WILMA. Then he can't do it. Don't let him do it. It's my house. It's all in this world that belongs to me. Let Mrs. Leighton take him if she wants to, but not my house. Please, please, please. (*She is crying. MINNA goes to her.*)

MINNA. Now, come on, honey. Come on, baby...

WILMA. I wouldn't sell it, not even to get me to Hollywood. I thought this afternoon, before the letter from Mr. Delafonte came, I'd ask Aunt Gert to let me sell it, and go on off, but when I went over there and sat in my yard and rocked in my swing and thought of my mama and how lonesome the house looked since we moved away... I knew I couldn't... I knew I never would... I'd never go to Hollywood before I'd sell that house, and he can't... I won't let him. I won't let him.

MINNA. Now, honey... honey... Miss Gert, do you know anything about this?

GERT. (*Wiping her eyes.*) Minna, I don't. I heard at the card party that he was marrying Mrs. Leighton... but I heard nothing about Lester's selling the house...

MINNA. Well, can he?...

GERT. I don't know. I just never thought my brother, my own brother... Oh, I just can't stand things like this. You see, it's all so mixed up. I don't think there was anything said in writing about Wilma's having the house, but it was clearly Alice's intention. She called me in the room before Lester and made him promise just before she died that he would always have the house for Wilma...

MINNA. Well, why don't we find out?...

GERT. Well... I don't know how... I left a message for Lester. I can't reach him.

MINNA. I'd call Mr. Bill if I were you. He's a lawyer.

GERT. But, Minna, my brother.

MINNA. I'd call me a lawyer, brother or no brother. If you don't, I will. I'm not gonna have what belongs to this child stolen from her by Mr. Lester or anybody else...

GERT. All right. I will. I'll go talk to Bill. I'll find out what we can do legally.

(She starts out d. l. of the area. LESTER comes in u. c. of the area. MINNA sees him coming.)

MINNA. Miss Gert.

(GERT turns and sees him just as he gets inside the area.)

LESTER. Hello, Gert.

GERT. Hello, Lester.

LESTER. Hello, Wilma.

WILMA. Hello...

GERT. Wilma, I think you'd better leave...

WILMA. Yes'm... *(She starts out.)*

LESTER. Wait a minute, Gert. I've something to tell you all. I want Wilma to hear...

GERT. I think we know already. Go on, Wilma.

WILMA. Yes'm

(*WILMA leaves d. l. of the area. MINNA follows after her. A pause.*)

GERT. We've heard about the marriage, Lester.

LESTER. Oh, well. I'm sorry I couldn't be the one to tell you. We only decided this morning. There was a lot to do, a license and some business to attend to. I haven't told anyone. I don't know how the news got to you.

GERT. You didn't really expect them to keep quiet about it at the courthouse?

LESTER. Oh. Well, of course I didn't think about that. (*A pause.*) Well, the other thing is... You see... I've decided to sell the house.

GERT. I know. Wilma just found out about that, too.

LESTER. Oh. Well, I'll explain the whole thing to you. You see, I felt... (*GERT starts to cry.*) Now what's the matter with you, Gert?

GERT. To think that my brother, my own brother, would do something like this.

LESTER. Like what? After all it's my house, Gert.

GERT. There's some dispute about that. The least I think you could have done, the very least, was come to tell your own child.

LESTER. Well, I'm here now to do that. I only put it up for sale at noon today. I've nothing to hide or be ashamed of. The house is in my name. Sybil, Mrs. Leighton, doesn't like Harrison. You can't blame her. People have been rotten to her. We're moving to Houston. I'm selling this house to pay down on one in Houston. That'll belong to Wilma just the same, someday. Sybil's agreed to that, and Wilma will really get a better house in time. And we always want her to feel like it's her home, come and visit us summers... and like I say when something happens to me or Sybil the house will be hers...

GERT. That's not the point, Lester...

LESTER. What do you mean?

GERT. You know very well.

LESTER. I can't make a home for her over there, can I? She'll be grown soon and marrying and having her own house. I held on to this place as long as I could... Well, I'm not going to feel guilty about it...

GERT. I'm going to try to stop you, Lester...

LESTER. Now look, Gert. For once try and be sensible...

GERT. Legally I'm going to try and stop you. I'm going...

LESTER. Please, Gert...

GERT. ...to call Bill and tell him the whole situation and see what we can do. If we have any rights I'll take it to every court I can. Brother or no brother...

LESTER. Now look, don't carry on like this. Maybe I've handled it clumsily and if I have I'm sorry. I just didn't think... I should have, I know... but I...

GERT. That's right. You didn't think. You never do. Well, this time you're going to have to...

LESTER. Can't you look at it this way? Wilma is getting a better house and...

GERT. Maybe she doesn't want a better house. Maybe she just wants this one. But that isn't the point either. The sickening part is that you really didn't care what Wilma thought, or even stopped for a moment to consider if she had a thought. You've never cared about anyone or anything but yourself. Well, this time I won't let you without a fight. I'm going to a lawyer.

LESTER. Gert...

GERT. Now get out of my house. Because brother or no, I'm through with you.

LESTER. All right. If you feel that way.

(*He leaves u. c. of the area. GERT stands for a moment, thinking what to do next. MINNA comes in d. l. of the area.*)

MINNA. I was behind the door and I heard the whole thing.

GERT. Did Wilma hear?

MINNA. No, I sent her back to her room. Now you get right to a lawyer.

GERT. I intend to. He's gotten me mad now. I won't let him get by with it if I can help it. I think I'll walk over to Bill's. I don't like to talk about it over the telephone.

MINNA. Yes'm.

GERT. You tell Wilma to wait here for me.

MINNA. Yes'm. Want me to tell her where you've gone?

GERT. I don't see why not. I'll be back as soon as I finish.

MINNA. Yes'm. (*GERT leaves u. c. of the area. MINNA goes to the door and calls:*) Wilma. Wilma. You can come here now. (*She fills a plate with food and puts it on the table. WILMA comes in d. l. of the area.*) You better sit down and try to eat something.

WILMA. I can't eat a thing.

MINNA. Well, you can try.

WILMA. No. It would choke me. What happened?

MINNA. Your aunt told him not to sell the house, and he said he would, and so she's gone to see a lawyer.

WILMA. Does she think she can stop him?

MINNA. She's gonna try. I know she's got him scared...

WILMA. But it's my house. You know that. He knows that... Didn't she tell him?

MINNA. Sure she told him. But you know your daddy. Telling won't do any good, we have to prove it.

WILMA. What proof have we got?

MINNA. Miss Gert's word. I hope that's enough...

WILMA. And if it isn't?

MINNA. Then you'll lose it. That's all. You'll lose it.

WILMA. I bet I lose it. I've got no luck.

MINNA. Why do you say that?

WILMA. What kind of luck is it takes your mama away, and then your daddy, and then tries to take your house. Sitting in that yard swinging I was the happiest girl in the world this afternoon. I'd decided not to go in the movies and to stay in Harrison and get married and have children and live in my house...

MINNA. Well, losing a house won't stop you from staying in Harrison and getting married...

WILMA. Oh, yes. I wouldn't trust it with my luck. With my kind of luck I wouldn't even get me a husband... I'd wind up like Miss Martha working at the post office chasing Mr. Russell Walter until the end of time. No mother and no father and no house and no husband and no children. No, thank you. I'm just tired of worrying over the whole thing. I'll just go on into Houston and see Mr. Delafonte and get on out to Hollywood and make money and get rich and famous. (*She begins to cry.*)

MINNA. Now, honey. Honey...

WILMA. Minna, I don't want to be rich and famous... I want to stay here. I want to stay in Harrison...

MINNA. Now, honey. Try to be brave.

WILMA. I know what I'm gonna do. (*She jumps up.*) I'm going to see old lady Leighton. She's the one that can stop this...

MINNA. Now, Wilma. You know your aunt don't want you around that woman.

WILMA. I can't help it. I'm going...

MINNA. Wilma... you listen to me... (*WILMA runs out u. c. of the area.*) Wilma... Wilma... you come back here...

(*But WILMA has gone. MINNA shakes her head in desperation. The lights fade. When the lights are brought up it is two hours later. MINNA is at the kitchen table reading the paper, GERT comes in u. c. of the area.*)

GERT. Well, we've won.

MINNA. What do you mean?

GERT. I mean just what I say. Lester is not going to sell the house.

MINNA. What happened?

GERT. I don't know what happened. I went over to see Bill and we talked it all through, and he said legally we really had no chance but he'd call up Lester and try to at least bluff him into thinking we had. And when he called Lester he said Lester wasn't home, and so I suggested his calling you know where.

MINNA. No. Where?

GERT. Mrs. Leighton's. And sure enough he was there, and then Bill told him why he was calling and Lester said well, it didn't matter as he'd decided not to sell the house after all.

MINNA. You don't mean it?

GERT. Oh, yes, I do. Where's Wilma?

MINNA. She's over there with them.

GERT. Over where with them?

MINNA. At Mrs. Leighton's.

GERT. Why, Minna...

MINNA. Now don't holler at me. I told her not to go, but she said she was going and then she ran out that door so fast I couldn't stop her.

(*WILMA comes running in u. c. of the area.*)

WILMA. Heard the news? House is mine again.

MINNA. Do you know what happened?

WILMA. Sure. Mrs. Leighton isn't so bad. Boy, I went running over there expecting the worst...

GERT. Wilma, what do you mean going to that woman's
house? Wilma, I declare...

WILMA. Oh, she's not so bad. Anyway, we've got her to
thank for it.

MINNA. Well, what happened? Will somebody please tell
me what happened?

WILMA. Well, you know I was sitting here and it came to
me. It came to me just like that. See Mrs. Leighton. She's
the one to stop it and it's got to be stopped. Well, I was
so scared my knees were trembling the whole time
going over there, but I made myself do it, walked in on
her and she looked more nervous than I did.

GERT. Was your father there?

WILMA. No ma'm. He came later. Wasn't anybody there
but me and Mrs. Leighton. I'm calling her Sybil now.
She asked me to. Did Arabella come yet?

MINNA. Arabella?

WILMA. I called and asked her to come and celebrate. I'm
so excited. I just had to have company tonight. I know

I won't be able to sleep anyway. I hope you don't mind, Aunt Gert....

MINNA. If you don't tell me what happened...

WILMA. Well... Mrs. Leighton... I mean Sybil... (*ARABELLA comes in u. c. of the area. WILMA sees her.*) Oh, come on in, Arabella.

ARABELLA. Hi. I almost didn't get to come. I told my mama it was life or death and so she gave in. But she made me swear we'd be in bed by ten. Did you hear about Mr. Delafonte?

WILMA. No? What?

ARABELLA. He's a crook. It was in the Houston papers tonight. He was operating a business under false pretenses. He had been charging twenty-five dollars for those screen tests and using a camera with no film in it.

WILMA. My goodness.

ARABELLA. It was in all the papers. On the second page. My father said he mustn't have been very much not to even get on the front page. He wasn't a Hollywood director at all. He didn't even know Lila Lee or Betty Compson.

WILMA. He didn't?

ARABELLA. No.

MINNA. Wilma, will you get back to your story before I lose my mind?

WILMA. Oh. Yes... I got my house back, Arabella.

ARABELLA. You did?

WILMA. Sure. That's why I called you over to spend the night. A kind of celebration.

ARABELLA. Well, that's wonderful.

MINNA. Wilma...

WILMA. All right. Where was I?

GERT. You were at Mrs. Leighton's.

WILMA. Oh, yes. Sibyl's. I'm calling her Sibyl now, Arabella. She asked me to.

MINNA. Well... what happened? Wilma, if you don't tell me...

WILMA. Well, I just told her the whole thing.

MINNA. What whole thing?

WILMA. Well, I told her about my mother meaning for the house to always be mine, and how I loved the house, and how I was lonely and the house was lonely and that I hoped my daddy and I could go there and live some-day but knew now we couldn't and that I planned to go to Hollywood and be a movie star but that this afternoon my friend Arabella and I decided we didn't really want to do that, and that I knew then that what I wanted to do really was to live in Harrison and get married and live in my house and have children so that I wouldn't be lonely anymore and the house wouldn't. And then she started crying.

GERT. You don't mean it.

WILMA. Yes ma'm. And I felt real sorry for her and I said I didn't hold anything against her and then Daddy came in, and she said why didn't he tell her that was my house, and he said because it wasn't. And then she asked him about what Mother told you, and he said that was true but now I was going to have a better house, and she said I didn't want to have a better house, but my own house, and that she wouldn't marry him if he sold this house and she said they both had jobs in Houston and would manage somehow, but I had nothing, so then he said all right.

GERT. Well. Good for her.

MINNA. Sure enough, good for her.

WILMA. And then Mr. Bill called and Daddy told him the house was mine again and then she cried again and hugged me and asked me to kiss her and I did, and then Daddy cried and I kissed him, and then I cried. And they asked me to the wedding and I said I'd go and that I'd come visit them this summer in Houston. And then I came home.

MINNA. Well. Well, indeed.

GERT. My goodness. So that's how it happened. And you say Mrs. Leighton cried?

WILMA. Twice. We all did. Daddy and Mrs. Leighton and me...

GERT. Well. I'm glad, Wilma, It's all worked out.

WILMA. And can I go visit them this summer in Houston?

GERT. If you like.

WILMA. And can I go to the wedding?

GERT. Yes, if you want to.

WILMA. I want to.

MINNA. Now you better have some supper.

WILMA. No. I couldn't eat, I'm still too excited.

MINNA. Miss Gert, she hasn't had a bite on her stomach.

GERT. Well, it won't kill her this one time, Minna.

WILMA. Aunt Gert, can Arabella and I go over to my yard for just a few minutes and swing? We'll be home by ten...

GERT. No, Wilma, it's late.

WILMA. Please. Just to celebrate. I have it coming to me. We'll just stay for a few minutes.

GERT. Well...

WILMA. Please...

GERT. Will you be back here by ten, and not make me have to send Minna over there?

WILMA. Yes ma'm.

GERT. All right.

WILMA. Oh, thank you. (*She goes to her aunt and kisses her.*) You're the best aunt in the whole world. Come on, Arabella.

ARABELLA. All right.

(*They start u. c. of the area. GERT calls after them:*)

GERT. Now remember. Back by ten. Arabella has promised her mother. And you've promised me.

WILMA. (*Calling in distance.*) Yes ma'm.

(*GERT comes back into the room.*)

GERT. Well, I'm glad it's ending this way.

MINNA. Yes ma'm.

GERT. I never thought it would. Well, I said hard things to Lester. I'm sorry I had to, but I felt I had to.

MINNA. Of course you did.

GERT. Well, I'll go to my room. You go on when you're ready.

MINNA. All right. I'm ready now. The excitement has wore me out.

GERT. Me too. Leave the light on for the children. I'll keep awake until they come in.

MINNA. Yes'm.

GERT. Good night.

MINNA. Good night.

> (*GERT goes out d. l. of the area. MINNA goes to get her hat. The lights fade. The lights are brought up in the d. r. area. WILMA and ARABELLA come in u. c. of the area and get in the swing.*)

WILMA. Don't you just love to swing?

ARABELLA. Uh huh.

WILMA. It's a lovely night, isn't it? Listen to that mocking-bird. The crazy thing must think it's daytime.

ARABELLA. It's light enough to be day.

WILMA. It certainly is.

ARABELLA. Well, it was lucky we decided to give up Hollywood with Mr. Delafonte turning out to be a crook and all.

WILMA. Wasn't it lucky?

ARABELLA. Do you feel lonely now?

WILMA. No, I don't feel nearly so lonely. Now I've got my house and plan to get married. And my daddy and I are going to see each other, and I think Mrs. Leighton is going to make a nice friend. She's crazy about moving pictures.

ARABELLA. Funny how things work out.

WILMA. Very funny.

ARABELLA. Guess who called me on the telephone.

WILMA. Who?

ARABELLA. Tommy... Murray.

WILMA. You don't say.

ARABELLA. He asked me for a date next week. Picture show. He said Jay was going to call you.

WILMA. Did he?

ARABELLA. I asked him to tell Jay that you weren't only interested in going out with movie actors.

WILMA. What did he say?

ARABELLA. He said he thought Jay knew that. (*A pause.*

WILMA jumps out of the swing.) Wilma. What's the matter with you? Wilma... (*She runs to her.*)

WILMA. I don't know. I felt funny for a minute. A cloud passed over the moon and I felt lonely... and funny... and scared...

ARABELLA. But you have your house now.

WILMA. I know... I... (*A pause. She points offstage r.*) I used to sleep in there. I had a white iron bed. I remember one night Aunt Gert woke me up. It was just turning light out, she was crying, "I'm taking you home to live with me," she said. "Why?" I said. "Because your mama's gone to heaven," she said. (*A pause.*) I can't remember my mama's face anymore. I can hear her voice sometimes calling me far off: "Wilma, Wilma come home." Far off. But I can't remember her face. I try and I try, but finally I have to go to my bureau drawer and take out her picture and look to remember... Oh, Arabella. It isn't only the house I wanted. It's the life in the house. My mama and me and even my daddy coming in at four in the morning...

ARABELLA. But there'll be life again in the house.

WILMA. How?

ARABELLA. You're gonna fill it with life again, Wilma. Like you said this afternoon.

WILMA. But I get afraid.

ARABELLA. Don't be. You will. I know you will.

WILMA. You think I can do anything. Be a movie star... Go to Hollywood. (*A pause.*) The moon's from behind the cloud. (*A pause. In the distance we can hear the court-house clock strike ten.*) Don't tell me it's ten o'clock already. I'll fill this house with life again. I'll meet a young man with steady ways and nice habits... (*Far off AUNT GERT calls: "Wilma. Wilma." WILMA calls back:*) We're coming. You see that pecan tree out there?

ARABELLA. Uh huh.

WILMA. It was planted the year my mother was born. It's so big now, I can hardly reach around it. (*AUNT GERT calls again: "Wilma. Wilma." WILMA calls back:*) We're coming.

(*She and ARABELLA sit swinging. WILMA looks happy and is happy as the lights fade.*)

Your Writing Assignment:

Here is the writing assignment I promised you. Use the following blank pages to talk about your gut responses to the play — what moved you? What are your strongest lingering impressions? Then I want you to write a general description of the circumstances presented in the play — What is the play basically about? Finally, write about the characters and, in a simple way, describe what each character's main concerns are in the play. Do this now and then move on to the next chapter in the book.

A man's most open actions have a secret side to them.
Joseph Conrad

c h a p t e r   f o u r

approaching the script

As we begin to work on this thing called interpretation, it is important that you understand, for us actors, the script is our bible. I am telling you that everything you decide about playing a part must be firmly based on what the playwright has given you in the text. If I were to ask you to show me how you made a particular choice and you could not prove to me how the script led you to that choice, than you have no right to it. It's all in the script. The script is the bedrock; it is our source of inspiration and serves as the catapult for our creative imagination.

So as we turn to the script and begin to examine the characters living in the imaginary circumstances created by the playwright, there are a few basic components we must be aware of which will show up in every well-written play.

85

Let's discuss the three essentials:

1) DESIRE:
Hunger, Appetite, Longing, Craving, Urge, Will, Zeal

How do those words affect you? Just reading those words immediately gets things stirring down in my gut. For you too? I say that you and I have a deep-seated understanding of this thing called desire. We wake up with it, it lurks behind our every move, it manifests itself in an infinite variety of actions, it colors all of our behavior, and whether in a whisper or a scream, it speaks to us as we wait to fall asleep. Let's call it our "deeper wish."

Every character in every play is born with this quality as well. Every well-written character has a profound hunger that shapes the things they say, the things they do, how they respond to the people around them and to the environment created by the circumstances of the play. It is vital then that we come to terms with the specific nature of the character's desire. You see, every character must be grappled with in a completely human way or the results will be false.

We call this aspect of the character, "the spine." Now, using the spine as an acting term is a great analogy because, literally, we know that for you and I, all human impulses travel through our bony structure called the spine and that the actual state of our spine has a great effect on the quality of our lives. The same is true as we take on the life of the character in the play because when we have a true connection to his or her "spine," we have something to measure the quality of our life on stage, how near or far we are from fulfilling our "deeper wish" in each moment. There it is again, my favorite definition of "spine" — the *"deeper wish."* Others may call the spine the "major objective," the "through-line," the "chief motivation," or the "arc" of the character. But I find all of those descriptions too technical and cold, none of them do it for me like "deeper wish." I love that phrase because first, it has the implication of how utterly private and personal this desire is, and second, it is absolutely active and inherently leads to action.

This is crucial. The spine is not only the character's specific desires, it is also his or her *"active response"* to that deeper wish. The same is true for you and me. And, if we are going to try to understand the spine of characters in plays, I believe it is important to wrestle with what our own spine in life is. So take some time right now to do the following writing assignment:

> I want you to write about what is it that you long for? What gets you out of bed every morning and injects you into your life? What "drives" you? Really look at and write about the things you have done in your life up until this point, the things you are doing in your life right now, and the things you hope to do and to have happen in the future. Paint a written picture of your own "spine," your own "deeper wish." After you have written about all of these things, try to sum up your desires into a simple, specific and short "spine phrase."

Listen, this is a difficult task and you will need to keep digging. Each time you come up with what you think is your true deeper wish and you sum it up into a spine phrase, ask yourself, *"Well, why that?"* For instance, you may say your spine phrase is:

"I want to be an actor."

Then ask yourself,

"Well, why that?"

Let's say you respond,

"Because I want to become famous and successful."

Ask yourself again,

"Well, why that?"

Let's say you respond,

"Because I want to be able to reach millions of people."

Ask yourself again,

"Well, why that?"

Get the idea? This process will help you get to the core of your own, very personal hunger. Take some time to do this writing assignment right now:

_____

_____

_____

_____

_____

_____

_____

_____

_____

_____

_____

_____

_____

_____

_____

_____

_____

_____

_____

_____

_____

_____

_____

_____

_____

_____

_____

_____

_____

_____

_____

_____

_____

Spine Phrase:_____

We will come back and talk more about the spine when we get to chapter eight, in which we will be working on becoming passionately and specifically active on stage. Now, let's move on to the second essential component.

2) URGENCY:
Seriousness, Insistence, Pressure, Importance, Necessity, Emergency

One of my great teachers, Suzanne Shepherd (who I've mentioned to you before) said it best,

For an actor, the answer to the question, "What time is it?" is always, *"Right Now!"*

The fact is that in all well-written plays the characters need to achieve something deeply personal, right now. Not next week, not tomorrow, NOW! Look at Wilma. When does she need to stop her father from selling the house? Next Tuesday? Later this afternoon? Remember the following moment in the play?

WILMA. I know what I'm gonna do. (*She jumps up.*) I'm going to see old lady Leighton. She's the one who can stop this...

MINNA. Now, Wilma. You know your aunt don't want you around that woman.

Do you remember Wilma's response? Does she say, "You know Minna, you're right. I'll stay here and wait to see what happens with Aunt Gert and if she can get my daddy to change his mind." NO SHE DOESN'T! Wilma's response is:

WILMA. I can't help it. I'm going...

MINNA. Wilma... you listen to me... (*WILMA runs out u. c. of the area.*) Wilma... Wilma... you come back here...

Get it? There is a necessity to take action and the pressure to accomplish something vital RIGHT NOW.

3) HIGH STAKES:
Imperative, Essential, Crucial, Critical, Inescapable

Here's another great quote from Suzanne:

Theater is never casual, it is always
EMERGENCY! EMERGENCY! EMERGENCY!

So acting is not only doing, it is meaningful doing. It is doing what is essential and crucial to us. Then we are led, naturally, organically, to the state of urgency we have just talked about; where it becomes absolutely imperative that we take action right now because the need to do so is inescapable.

How about you? I want you to write about a time when the stakes were high for you. Write what the circumstances were and talk about your "active response" to your deeply held need in those moments? Do that now:

_____

_____

_____

_____

_____

_____

_____

_____

_____

_____

A wise man hears one word and understands two.
Yiddish Proverb

chapter five
the key phrase

All right, let's get to work on our exploration of playing Wilma in *A Young Lady of Property.* In order to do so, the first thing I want you to know is that it is not possible to read the play too much. As for me, when I play a part, I am continually reading the play, over and over and over again. Hundreds of times. I carry the play with me everywhere I go and any free moment I find, I am back in that script. It is my strong suggestion that you do the same.

The next phase of the work will be to begin the process of bringing you and the words of the playwright into a more specific relationship; bringing yourself into a personal, inner alignment with the "point of view" of the character. Let's stop here for a moment so that I can highlight a very important ingredient: *point of view.*

Simply, point of view as how we "see" the world; it is the meaning we assign to the people and events in our world and how we respond to these people and events. Truly, our "character" is defined by our own point of view because it is this point of view that is the driving force behind all of our behavior. The same holds true for the "character" in the play. It is essential then, that we find a way not only to define the point of view of the character in the play, but that we work in such a way that we actually begin to "see" through the eyes of the character; that we see from the character's vantage point with the *"eyes of our heart."*

I must tell you, there has to be a falling-in-love process here. If I haven't said this to you before, I will say it now. If you can not fall in love with the character you play, you cannot play him or her. And sometimes, the character's point of view will be vastly different than your own. Still, you must find your way in. Did you hear that? You must find your way in. And in this effort, you are forced to uncover the characters humanity. It's really your only shot at bringing life to the stage.

I want to give you a two-part writing assignment that I give to all of my in-person students and to my readers. This exercise will help you explore your own point of view. (Which many people never really do. But which, for actors, is vital.) You may even find the following assignments useful as something to continue doing in journal form, with a daily or weekly entry.

Do the assignment now and then continue with the book.

Get a current newspaper or magazine. Find an article that makes you furious, absolutely enraged. Cut the article out and tape it on to this page. Then, write about why you chose it and what it means to you, on the following page.

Tape Article Here

Write About Article Here

_____

_____

_____

_____

_____

_____

_____

_____

_____

_____

_____

_____

_____

_____

_____

_____

_____

_____

_____

_____

_____

_____

_____

_____

_____

_____

_____

_____

_____

_____

Now find an article that makes you want to jump for joy, one that makes you happy to be alive! Tape the article on to this page and write your responses to it on the following page.

Tape Article Here

Write About Article Here

_____

_____

_____

_____

_____

_____

_____

_____

_____

_____

_____

_____

_____

_____

_____

_____

_____

_____

_____

_____

_____

_____

_____

_____

_____

_____

_____

Reading the play over and over and over again was really your first step in becoming acquainted with the point of view of the character. The next step in uncovering and honing in on the point of view of the character is the use of what I call the key phrases.

These phrases are things the character says that you feel are of true importance to him or her.

As you choose the key phrases, you will begin to clarify how the character perceives the world and what his or her deeply held wants and needs are.

So here's your next assignment in working on Wilma. I want you to read the play again. This time, as you go through it, pick out the things Wilma says that you think are truly important to her. Remember, these are not just "any old thing" she says, these are KEY phrases. As you find these phrases, write them here in the book. Make sure to use Wilma's exact words. Do not paraphrase her words, do not describe how you feel about what she is saying, and do not comment on what you think she feels about what she is saying. Simply write down exactly what she does say.

Sometimes the key phrase might be a brief exchange between Wilma and another character. That's okay, write it down. Many times the key phrase will be only part of a line. Good, write it down. Anything that you believe is of great importance to Wilma and helps you understand her point of view, write it down. One more thing. If it is not clear in the phrase who or what Wilma is referring to, write who or what she is talking about directly next to the phrase, in parentheses.

Ready to work? Good, get started.

Wilma's Key Phrases

_____

_____

_____

_____

_____

_____

_____

_____

_____

_____

_____

_____

_____

_____

_____

_____

_____

_____

_____

_____

_____

_____

_____

_____

_____

_____

Here are the key phrases for Wilma that I pulled out of the script.

- somebody very important (Mr. Delafonte)

- they were tearing it to pieces (the tenants in her house)

- I'd like to scratch that old cat's eyes out (about Martha when Martha says Wilma's daddy will marry old lady Leighton)

- my mother left it to me (the house)

- my mother told aunt Gert it was mine just before she died

- I feel very lucky having my own house

- I own a house which is very unusual

- I'm a young lady of property

- Mama and I used to play croquet in the yard under the pecan trees

- my mama died of a broken heart

- Daddy's gambling broke her heart

- I've forgiven him (Daddy)

- I love him now (Daddy)

- I'd give up this whole movie star business if I could go back to our house and live with Daddy

- she's got my daddy hog-tied (Mrs. Leighton)

- Aunt Gert says she isn't good enough to shine my mother's shoes and I think she's right (Mrs. Leighton)

- Wilma: Do you like snakes?
  Arabella: No.
  Wilma: Well neither do I like Mrs. Leighton and for the same reason.

- He's giving screen tests to people of beauty and talent, and if they pass they'll go to Hollywood and be in the picture shows.

- come right over if I have a letter

- Mr. Delafonte the famous movie director

- I'll go to Hollywood and be a Wampus baby star

- if you mean my daddy and old lady Leighton, I'd burn it down first (about daddy and Mrs. Leighton living in Wilma's house)

- I'm scared my daddy is going to marry Mrs. Leighton

- let's pack our bags Hollywood here we come

- I'll never stop being your friend (to Arabella)

- I'm scared of lots of things...old lady Leighton taking my daddy away

- I'll always be your friend (to Arabella)

- I love to swing in my front yard. Mama and I used to come out here and swing together. I used to wake up and hear her out here swinging away. Sometimes she'd let me come and sit beside her.

- sometimes my old house looks so lonesome it tears at my heart

- it has looked lonesome ever since Mama died and we moved away

- it will look lonesome until some of us move back here

- until I meet some nice boy with good habits and steady ways and marry him

- then we'll move here and have children and I bet this old house won't be lonely anymore (speaking about getting married)

- maybe I was going to Hollywood out of pure lonesomeness

- I felt so alone with Mrs. Leighton getting my daddy and my mama having left the world

- Daddy could have taken away my lonesomeness but he didn't want to or couldn't

- I'll stay and marry and live in my house

- it's my house, it's all in this world that belongs to me

- let Mrs. Leighton take him if she wants to but not my house, please, please, please

- when I went over there and sat in my yard and rocked in my swing and thought of my mama and how lonesome the house looked since we moved away I knew I couldn't, I knew I never would (sell the house and go to Hollywood)

- I've got no luck. What kind of luck is it takes your mama away and then your daddy and then tries to take your house

- Minna, I don't want to be rich and famous, I want to stay here

- I can't remember my mama's face anymore

- it isn't only the house I wanted. It's the life in the house

Did you get most of the same phrases as I did? And, isn't it wonderful to go through the script and pull out these key phrases? There, right in front of you, you now have a very specific look at the most important things in Wilma's life at this moment and how she feels about them. We have clearly defined that the main areas of concern for Wilma are:

her house
her mama
her daddy
Mrs. Leighton
going to Hollywood

Of course, there are other things that are meaningful to Wilma. There is the idea of getting married to a certain kind of boy, and there are her relationships with Arabella, with Aunt Gert, and with Minna. But these are not really the *pressing and critical* areas of Wilma's current concerns. (In the next chapter, I will show you how to deal with all of these aspects of Wilma's life.)

To continue working on Wilma's point of view and her "deeper wish," I want you to read through your list of key phrases a few more times and pick out the ones that you feel are the *most "provocative" things she says:* the phrases which, when you read them, really do something to you down in your gut. As you find these provocative statements, write them down in the space below. Please do that now:

Most Provocative Statements

_____

_____

_____

_____

_____

_____

_____

_____

Here are the ones I chose:

- My mama died of a broken heart

- I love him now (daddy)

- I'd give up this whole movie star business if I could go back to our house and live with daddy

- I'm scared my daddy is going to marry Mrs. Leighton

- sometimes my old house looks so lonesome it tears at my heart

- it's my house, it's all in this world that belongs to me

- I can't remember mama's face anymore

- it isn't only the house I wanted, it's the life in the house

Can you see how this process really brings us to the heart of the matter?

For instance, all of the harsh and negative things Wilma says about Mrs. Leighton, some of which are clearly a repeat of things she has heard from the mouth of Aunt Gert, are really about one thing:

I'm scared my daddy is going to marry Mrs. Leighton

Don't you think, knowing all the things we know about Wilma, that this is a potent line? It is a line filled with all the horrors for Wilma, of not only having lost her mama, but now, having her daddy taken away from her as well.

So, what do we do with these provocative statements? As I said earlier, it is absolutely essential that we find a way to personally and authentically connect with the point of view of the character. In order to do that, I have a powerful writing exercise for you. If you do this process consistently, in the ways I will show you here and in the following chapters of this book, you will discover a wonderful and effective means of crawling inside the skin and into the heart of the character.

In a moment, I am going to ask you to:

1. Choose one of your provocative statements and write it at the top of a page here in the book. (I will give you four pages here in the book for four statements. Do any other provocative statements in your own writing journal.)

2. Then, as soon as you have written the statement down, I want you to close your eyes and say the statement to yourself (not out loud). Say it to yourself over and over for a good few minutes and do so in a relaxed manner. Simply allow the words to work on you.

3. After saying the statement to yourself, open your eyes and, immediately, directly underneath the statement, I want you to write a free association. By free association, what I mean is – do not censor anything – write whatever comes out of you as a result of saying the provocative statement to yourself and allowing it to work on you.

Two important things:

1. Write the free association *in first person.* I am not asking you to write as "Wilma," I am asking you to freely write your responses using the word "I" rather than "Wilma" or "she."

2. Once you begin writing, *do not stop or pause.* Do not use punctuation marks. Write swiftly and keep your pen going until you have filled the entire page. As an example, I will do one for you right now:

Provocative statement:
It's my house, it's all in the world that belongs to me

I have nothing much in this life but I have my house I don't really have a daddy even though I have one and I love him but does he love me I don't know I want him so bad to love me and to make a family with me but I don't think I can ever have a real family again I need a family I need my mommy I need my daddy I need someone to hold me and hug me and make it okay but I hurt my heart hurts and I am so sad and scared and worried that my life is over but I am so young and I have so much love in me and I want to give it all to my daddy but he doesn't really want it and he wants to get rid of my house and I am so alone but when I am in my house I feel my mama and I look at her picture and I know I am loved I still feel her love even though she's not here but I feel her near me when I am in my house and I see our swing and I imagine swinging with her still and that hurts so bad cause I miss my mama I miss her so much oh God I hurt I hurt god why did you take my mama away from me why did you abandon me and make my mama so sick I want my mama back I want to live in my house with my mama God I want to feel her hold me I want to hold her hand those long pretty fingers and walk out in the garden and smell the trees I want to be a child again and happy and without the dread I feel now God please don't let my daddy take my house from me please don't let my daddy take my mama away I have nothing else but my house and my mama I want her back God and I want to live in my house oh please make our life whole please God please...

I could have continued writing, but I wanted to give you a brief example of what this process looks like. I can tell you that the more I wrote, the more I felt deeply in pain and very alone. And now, when I say that line to myself *"It's my house, it's all in the world that belongs to me"* I have a very personal understanding and connection to those words that is not merely intellectual. Just saying those words makes my heart feel like it's going to crack open and like I can't get quite enough air to breathe. And don't you think, way down, underneath all of her words, very similar things are going on inside of Wilma?

If you look at what I wrote, you see clearly that my relationship with the whole play (a result of my reading the play and writing the key phrases) had a direct influence on my free association. This influence was out of my control. But did all the thoughts, feelings, and images of my free association come from Wilma? Did they come from Horton? No, they came from somewhere down in me.

You see, both are at work here. We have the inspiration of Horton's text and the original spark of life that lives within that text, which came from deep down in Horton. And, we have the wisdom from the part of us that knows more about playing this part than anything we can cook up in our heads. That wisdom lives deep down in us. And, if we are going to have that mysterious and indefinable part of our instrument lead us effectively, we must nourish and nurture it. That is exactly what we are doing with these key phrases, provocative statements, and the free-association form of writing based on the provocative statements.

Don't forget. What we are working on here is *taking on the point of view of the character in an authentic and personal way.* All right, now I want you to do it. Here again is the assignment:

Choose one of the provocative statements and write it at the top of a page here in the book.

As soon as you have written the statement down, close your eyes and say the statement to yourself for a few minutes in a relaxed manner. Allow the words to work on you.

Open your eyes and immediately write a free association underneath the statement.

Write the free association in first person, using the word "I" rather than "Wilma" or "she."

Once you begin writing, do not stop or pause. Do not use punctuation marks. Write swiftly and keep your pen going until you have filled the entire page.

Provocative Statement

_____

_____

_____

_____

_____

_____

_____

_____

_____

_____

_____

_____

_____

_____

_____

_____

_____

_____

_____

_____

_____

_____

_____

_____

_____

_____

_____

_____

_____

_____

Provocative Statement

_____
_____
_____
_____
_____
_____
_____
_____
_____
_____
_____
_____
_____
_____
_____
_____
_____
_____
_____
_____
_____
_____
_____
_____
_____
_____
_____
_____
_____
_____

Provocative Statement

_____

_____

_____

_____

_____

_____

_____

_____

_____

_____

_____

_____

_____

_____

_____

_____

_____

_____

_____

_____

_____

_____

_____

_____

_____

_____

_____

_____

_____

_____

_____

_____

Provocative Statement

_____

_____

_____

_____

_____

_____

_____

_____

_____

_____

_____

_____

_____

_____

_____

_____

_____

_____

_____

_____

_____

_____

_____

_____

_____

_____

_____

_____

_____

_____

_____

_____

_____

Before we do anything else, I want to tell you that you mustn't try to come to any conclusions yet. We are involved in building something and we are doing this in a step-by-step fashion. All I ask is that you actually do these assignments and that you allow these exercises to "work on you" in whatever fashion they do.

Please complete the work on the key phrases before you move on to chapter six so that you will have laid the groundwork for the things we will be doing next.

You must learn to be still in the midst of activity
and to be vibrantly alive in repose.
Indira Gandhi

c h a p t e r   s i x

the key fact

Previously, I talked with you at length about what is truly communicated from the stage and what the audience is actually receiving. I told you that acting is never about "showing," it is always about "knowing." As a way of introducing the work with "key facts," let's review what it means to really "know" something and how that relates to our acting.

First of all, many actors approach acting as a job where they get to stand on stage and be admired by others for how good they are at "making it look like" something is actually happening when the truth is, nothing is actually happening. We call this illustrating. It is the actor's attempt to convince the audience that there is something real going on when nothing real is going on. Want a simpler way of saying it? That actor is a liar. Why do so many actors lie in this manner? Because it's easy. And when these actors get real slick at it, they may win the approval of others, and sometimes, make lots of money. But you know what? You can't lie to an audience. No matter how good you are at it, they know — somewhere in them, they know. This is a problem that is also perpetuated by hordes of directors who shake in their boots when faced with an actor who struggles to work in an authentic way. Again, there is a price to pay if we are going to work in the way we have been grappling with in these books, there's no way around it; there is a high price and the cost is personal. Many actors are unwilling to pay that price and, certainly, there are fewer directors willing to do so.

Quickly now, read the first statement, fill in the blank, and then write about it. Don't stop writing until you have filled in all the blank lines:

The first person I fell in love with was _____
and I remember a beautiful time when we_____

_____

_____

_____

_____

_____

_____

_____

_____

_____

_____

_____

_____

_____

_____

_____

My question to you is, as you consider the things you just wrote down in response to the above statement, where did those responses come from?

Well, they came from that place in you (wherever it is), that really knows. All of us have that place, it is our center, our core of meaning. So, as you wrote, you were expressing something you really know about. If we were here together, and I asked you that question and you talked with me about it, I would see that meaning living in you. As you share with me this precious time in your life, I would see its meaning living in your eyes, I would see it in the ways your hands gesture and in your physical posture. I would hear that meaning in the sound of your voice and in your silences when you don't have the words. And, as you talked with me simply and authentically, all of this "behavior," would be happening without a trace, without a speck of effort on your part. This, my friends, is a crucial note for actors. So, I'll say it again. *As you talked with me simply and authentically, all of this "life" happening in you, would be happening without a trace, without a speck of effort on your part.*

Also, not only would I see and hear the meaning living in you, I would receive it in that secret place in me that is built to search for and embrace such things, and designed to relate such things to my own, human connection to the world. (You know, in class, I repeat things over and over and over. You're lucky because, in these books, I usually won't say things more than twice. Usually. And because we are reviewing right now and because this thing is so huge, I will repeat what I just said one more time. Hey, I'll even put it in italic letters...)

Not only would I see and hear the meaning living in you, I would receive it in that secret place in me that is built to search for and embrace such things and designed to relate such things to my own human connection to the world.

And this is exactly why the audience came to see the play tonight. Do you get that? Like you and I, they are hungry. That place in them built to search for, witness, and embrace authentic, human behavior is hungry! And no one can say a damn thing to make me feel otherwise. The audience has come because there is something essential that they are in search of; they come seeking something to reconnect them with their own humanity and with the possibility for genuine human relatedness. (Do you really think anyone pays a hundred bucks a seat to be lied to and to then forget about the show ten minutes after they leave?) Does your audience know consciously that they come hoping to have their life changed? Probably not. This doesn't make it untrue. I am telling you it is true. And, for me, if I didn't believe it, I couldn't go on with this thing another day.

On one level, the audience watching the show is receiving the story of the play that is communicated by the words the actors speak. In addition there is the influence of the physical production (sets, costumes, lighting, etc.). But when the actors have *personally invested* themselves into the circumstances of the play and into the text, the audience is also getting the "story" that is unseen, unstated, and that lives beneath the layer of the words. With the vehicle of personal meaning and human behavior, these courageous actors have paved the way to give birth to art that is more than entertaining, it is profoundly moving.

To conclude the review portion, I want to remind you of this great thing Peter Brook said:

> A word does not start as a word — it is an end product which begins as an impulse, stimulated by attitude and behavior which dictate the need for expression. This process occurs inside the dramatist; it is then repeated inside the actor. Both may only be conscious of the words, but both for the author and then for the actor, the word is a small visible portion of a gigantic unseen formation. Some writers attempt to nail down their meaning and intentions in stage directions and explanations, yet we cannot help being struck by the fact that the best dramatists explain themselves the least. They recognize that the only way to find the true path to the speaking of a word is through a process that parallels the original creative one. This can neither be bypassed nor simplified.

Mr. Brook is telling us that dialogue is really the last thing that occurs, it is the "end product," and that the speaking of words is always a result of what he calls the "need for expression." In my favorite line, he says, "the word is a small visible portion of a gigantic formation." It is precisely this formation that you are involved in generating as you do the work here in the book — a process that Brook says "can neither be bypassed nor simplified."

On to the Key Facts...

The work we have done with "key phrases" was a first phase of "knowing what you are talking about" on stage, and it was aimed at inhabiting the point of view of the character. But what about the personal history of the character and her relationship to the people and events in her life. Certainly, when the character speaks about these things, she knows what she is talking about. *But we don't.* Do you see that?

For example, when the words "old lady Leighton" come out of Wilma's mouth, she has an intimate connection with these words. She doesn't have to stop and imagine what old lady Leighton looks like because she knows that. She doesn't have to stop and consider what old lady Leighton means to her because she knows that too. And now, you are playing the part of Wilma and you have to say "old lady Leighton" and the thing is, you don't know what you are talking about. Isn't that true? Do you have a woman named "old lady Leighton" in your life who is about to marry your daddy? Probably not. Even if you did, she's not Wilma's old lady Leighton.

So how do you take the words spoken by the character and make them your own so that when you speak those words, you too, know what you are talking about? Well, in many acting classes, especially in the colleges, acting students are given an exercise to do that is, for the most part, useless. It is called, the character's "biography." *"Hey Smitty, do a biography on your character."* So what does Smitty do? He goes home and makes up all kinds of intellectually appealing facts about the character's past that the play doesn't give him: the hospital the character was born in, what blood type the character is, if the character had a dog when he was five, and so on... All of this is a tremendous waste of time. I mean, look, how is the blood type gonna help you act the part! Here's a great quote which speaks to this:

> Depend upon it, there comes a time when for every addition of knowledge you forget something that you knew before. It is of the highest importance, therefore, not to have useless facts elbowing out the useful ones.
>
> Sir Arthur Conan Doyle

What you need then is a way to work with the text that will result in a personal history for the character, that emerges from both you and the character. Why? So that when you speak the words of the script, you are speaking from what you truly know. Here's your next assignment. I want you to read the play again. This time you will pull out a list of "key facts."

The key facts are any person, place or thing that Wilma speaks about and that are significant to her.

For example, when Aunt Gert has the headache, Wilma says to Minna, *"If she wants any ice, I'll crack it."* Well, ice is a "thing" that Wilma mentions. But is it really significant in her life? Clearly it's not and I would not include "ice" in my list of key facts. How about Wilma's swing? Yes, obviously, that would be on my list of key facts. Enough talk, go ahead now and write down your key facts on the next page:

Wilma's Key Facts:

_____

_____

_____

_____

_____

_____

_____

_____

_____

_____

_____

_____

_____

_____

_____

_____

_____

_____

_____

_____

_____

_____

_____

_____

_____

_____

_____

_____

_____

_____

_____

Here is my list:
    Miss Martha
    Mr. Russell Walter
    Mr. Peter
    Arabella
    the tenants
    Cousin Neeley
    Aunt Gert
    Minna
    Daddy
    Mama
    my house
    the pecan tree
    croquet
    Daddy's gambling
    Mr. Delafonte
    the letter
    Mrs. Leighton
    "Sweet Alice Ben Bolt"
    being a movie star
    my swing
    lonesomeness
    getting married
    Mr. Mavis
    luck
    Harrison
    Jay Godfrey
    Tommy Murray
    typing & shorthand
    Wampus baby star
    white starched dresses
    Pola Negri
    Betty Compson
    Lila Lee
    the screen test
    a nice boy

Now that you have your list of key facts, the next thing you are to do is put each key fact on the top of its own page. I will give you four pages here in the book to use and I want you to use your own writing journal for the rest.

Also, when you write the key facts at the top of the pages in your journal, only use the front of each page. (You will need the blank space on the front and back of each page to do writing assignments based on each key fact.)

Go ahead now and do that.

When you're done, go on to the your next assignment.

Key Fact:

_____

_____

_____

_____

_____

_____

_____

_____

_____

_____

_____

_____

_____

_____

_____

_____

_____

_____

Key Fact:

_____
_____
_____
_____
_____
_____
_____
_____
_____
_____
_____
_____
_____
_____
_____
_____
_____
_____
_____
_____
_____
_____
_____
_____
_____
_____
_____

128 playing the part

Key Fact:

_____
_____
_____
_____
_____
_____
_____
_____
_____
_____
_____
_____
_____
_____
_____
_____
_____
_____
_____
_____
_____
_____
_____
_____
_____
_____
_____
_____

Key Fact:

_____
_____
_____
_____
_____
_____
_____
_____
_____
_____
_____
_____
_____
_____
_____
_____
_____
_____
_____
_____
_____
_____
_____
_____
_____
_____
_____
_____
_____
_____
_____

The next thing you will do is take each key fact, one at a time, go back to the script, and find everything Wilma says about that key fact. As you find the things she says, you will write down everything that supports Wilma's "true point of view" toward that key fact. For instance, let's imagine that Wilma was very frustrated with Arabella for a moment and she said to Minna, *"That Arabella is a worthless little fool."* Would you write that down? No you wouldn't. Why? Because we know, from everything else we get in the script, that this line does not support Wilma's true point of view toward Arabella.

Here's an example of what I want you to do, using one of the key facts I chose:

KEY FACT: the tenants
They were asked to leave because they were tearing it to pieces. They had weeds growing in the yards and had torn off wallpaper. My Aunt Gert asked them to leave. I think I'll go over and see my house, look at how those tenants left it. I can't ever go over there when there's tenants living in it.

Do you see how by picking out and writing down Wilma's words about the key fact directly underneath that fact, you now have a snapshot of Wilma's relationship with that key fact?

Now, you do the work.

I want you to go back to your pages with the key facts (including the pages here in the book and the ones in your journal) and take the time to go through the play completely for each key fact that you chose. Work with one key fact at a time. As you do, write down everything Wilma says that supports her true point of view toward that key fact. Take whatever time you need to complete all of your key facts and then move on to the next, key-fact assignment.

. . .

Have you completed extracting what Wilma says about all the key facts from the play in the manner I described?

Really?

You wouldn't kid me, would you?

(I am trying to impress upon you that the value in this book is in "doing it!")

Similar to the free-association form of writing you did with the provocative statements in the previous chapter, in a moment, you are going to be writing free associations based on the key facts and on what Wilma has said about each one. The way I want you to do this is to, first, go back to the page with the first key fact you chose. Then, read the key fact to yourself and read everything you wrote down beneath it. Then, I want you to allow that reading to kick you off into writing a free association. (Wherever Wilma's own words about the key fact end on your page, that's where I want you to begin writing your free association.) Again, write quickly, without punctuation and without pausing. And, rather than filling the whole page, simply write a paragraph or so.

Before I have you begin writing, using the example of the key fact I used earlier, I will show you what this looks like:

KEY FACT: the tenants

They were asked to leave because they were tearing it to pieces. They had weeds growing in the yards and had torn off wall paper. My Aunt Gert asked them to leave. I think I'll go over and see my house, look at how those tenants left it. I can't ever go over there when there's tenants living in it these last tenants were the worst that big fat man he couldn't even fit through the bathroom door and he put a crack in the wall that will need to be repaired and those bratty two daughters of his but i do feel sad for him all the same not having a wife and all but i still can't forgive the way those kids ripped up the wallpaper in my old room the lilacs that were so pretty to look at when i'd lay in bed and mama worked so hard to put up for me that her fingers hurt and even though they have been out of the house for a week the place still has the smell of whiskey that man sure drank a lot and I hope I never have to rent it again but i am afraid i will have to and we will fix the place up for them and they will wreck it just like these folks did

That's is my first installment of working with that particular key fact. Even after this initial bit of writing, I discovered some specific things about the tenants that I didn't know before. As I wrote in the form of a true, free association, information showed up on my page that is much more wonderful than any clever thing I could have come up with in my head. Did you hear what I just said? Let me highlight the crucial part: *"information showed up."* Where did all this information come from. It came from somewhere in me that "knows."

Now, I have a relationship with the words "the tenants." I don't even have to go back and read what I wrote because I already know inside me that this extremely obese man, an alcoholic, lived there without a wife and with two daughters. And, I uncovered a number of specific things:

- I know that the obese man put a crack in the wall because he had a hard time fitting through the bathroom door

- I know that I had lilac wallpaper in my bedroom and it was this wallpaper that the two daughters destroyed.

- I know that I have even felt bad for that family, not having a mom, but this does not diminish my anger about the wallpaper being torn up.

- I know that my mother worked hard on the wallpaper in my room and I remember how her fingers ached when she put the wallpaper up.

- I know I loved to look at the lilacs when I was in bed.

- I know that the house still stinks from the man's whiskey.

- My question to you is, when I act the scene, what do I do with all these things I discovered about the tenants?

The answer is:

I don't do anything with them. I simply know them.

Why? Because when I have to say those words, "the tenants," I really do know what I am talking about. Listen, the information about the tenants came from a nonintellectual place in me, rather than from any highbrow ideas I could have tried to make in my head, so the things I discovered about the tenants truly do live in me. And, when I have to speak the words, "the tenants" in the scene, these words will come from that place of meaning in me: meaning that will have it's own, organic impact on my behavior. Most importantly:

As I act, authentic human behavior, rich in personal meaning, will occur with no effort on my part.

These free associations are a powerful tool and the more you work with them, the more you will find yourself getting out of your own way. Do you remember that profound thing D'Vorah shared with us early on?

I am a vessel. And if I can really open up, something greater than me will come through me.

That's a useful reminder. (Thanks again to D'Vorah!)

One more thing.

Another nice payoff of the writing I did on this key fact is that I made clear for myself what Wilma means when she says *"I think I'll go over and see my house, look at how those tenants left it."* At first, I might think after reading that line that she has not seen the house since the tenants have moved out. But Wilma also says, *"They had weeds growing in the yards and had torn off wallpaper."* So I wonder, did Wilma hear about what happened at the house from Aunt Gert or has Wilma been in the house herself? From my writing, Wilma has clearly been in the house and witnessed all these things. So now, the meaning of the line, *"I think I'll go over and see my house, look at how those tenants left it."* does not mean that Wilma hasn't been in the house, it means something like *"I feel so rotten about my poor house. I simply have to get back over there and look at it again. I just need to be there right now."*

What incredible gifts that one bit of writing gave to me. Don't you think?

What would I do next?

I would do the writing exercise I just did for the key fact, "the tenants," with all of the key facts. And, I would do it at one sitting. Then, tomorrow, I would do the same. I would read each key fact to myself, read everything written underneath that key fact, and then I would allow the words to kick me off into another paragraph of free associating. Then, the next day, I would do the same thing again. I would do this process until I had filled up the front and back of every key fact page in my journal. In this way, over time, I would establish a very specific and personal relationship with all the people, places, and things that are significant in Wilma's life. I'm telling you, this work is dynamic and persuasive!

Here's your assignment:

- Work with each key fact, one at a time.

- Read the key fact to yourself, read everything you wrote down beneath it and then allow that to kick you off into writing a free association.

- Wherever Wilma's words about the key fact end on your page, that's where I want you to begin writing your free association.

- Write quickly, without punctuation and without pausing.

- Rather than filling the whole page, simply write a paragraph or so for each key fact at this writing session. And do all the key facts, in this manner, at this sitting.

- Each day, have a writing session for all the key facts. Do this until you have filled the entire front and back of each page. Simply read the key fact and everything previously written under the key fact and allow it to get you started on a new free association.

- When you have completed at least one session of writing for all of the key facts, move on to the next chapter in this book. And, as you work on the next chapter, continue your daily writing sessions with the key facts.

The ordinary man is involved in action, the hero acts.
An immense difference.
Henry Miller

chapter seven

taking on the part

Slowly, step-by-step, we have been approaching and making connections with this thing we call "the character." In our case, of course, the character is "Wilma." Sandy told us acting is doing and he defined character as *"how you do what you do."* Unfortunately, many actors believe that the *how* in "how you do what you do," is playing the part with a limp or a stutter or some other physical impediment. So those actors do a limp and think they've made a character when all that they have accomplished is making a limp. What do you think they left out? Hmmm... could it be "the person"? Shouldn't someone remind these actors that there is supposed to be a human being who is living with that limp?

And, yes... yes... of course... If I am a person who walks through life with a limp, certainly, I am going to be deeply influenced by that physical condition. But the impediment is not the "root" and it is the root we have to get at.

140

What then is the root of "character"? What is the source of "how we do what we do"? What do you think it is? I'll give you a hint, it's three words. Fill in the blank:

The source of character is _____

Did you say "Simon and Garfunkle"? How about, "Donny and Marie"? Uh... "Gumby and Pokey"? Really, Tara? You said Gumby and Pokey? Well, maybe some of you said "point of view." If you did, you got it right. Yes, the source of character, the thing that will shape "how" you do what you do is point of view. Remember, as we established earlier, point of view is your gut level response to the people and circumstances that make up your life. (Now, if you decide to give your character a physical impediment or if it is required by the demands of the script, the vital question for you, the actor is, *How does this condition shape how I "view" the world"?* Of course, this question cannot be answered intellectually. It must be answered through a process of "living" with that physical condition, continually allowing the physical condition to "feed" that deeper place within ourselves.)

So if the origins of character reside in a person's specific attitudes toward the people and circumstances all around him or her, don't you think we have made a great investment by doing all of the work we have done up until this point? I say yes. Everything we have been working on, and which we will continue to work on in this chapter, is about deepening the source of character. And, that's not the end of the story! All of this work is only fulfilled — "character" is only realized — when we fully immerse ourselves in "taking action," which is the subject of chapter eight.

As F. Scott Fitzgerald said:

Action is character.

Up until now, everything you have been doing has been a process called "personalization" or, making the text "your own." And all of the work has prepared you to do the next form of personalization, which will be more specifically about "taking on the part." In order to teach you the next part of the process, I will be taking some of Wilma's lines from the scene we are working on and I will delete some words. I will also delete Arabella's responses so that we have an uninterrupted speech spoken by Wilma to work with. Here it is:

> I love to swing in my front yard. Aunt Gert has a swing in her front yard, but it's not the same. Mama and I used to come out here and swing together. Some nights when Daddy was out all night gambling, I used to wake up and hear her out here swinging away. Sometimes she'd let me come and sit beside her. We'd swing until three or four in the morning. The pear tree looks sickly, doesn't it? The fig trees are doing nicely though. I was out in the back and the weeds are near knee high, but fig trees just seem to thrive in the weeds. The freeze must have killed off the banana trees... Maybe I won't leave either. Maybe I won't go to Hollywood after all. That just comes to me now. You know sometimes my old house looks so lonesome it tears at my heart. I used to think it looked lonesome just whenever it had no tenants, but now it comes to me it has looked lonesome ever since Mama died and we moved away, and it will look lonesome until some of us move back here. Of course, Mama can't, and Daddy won't. So it's up to me.

Let's go back into Studio Five, where I am in class and working with Nyle Lynn. I want you, the reader, to pay very close attention now...

(Nyle Lynn, who prefers to be called "Nyle," is sitting on an old wooden chair in front of the group. She is working on the scene here in class and playing the part of Wilma. She has done all the work that you have been doing with the key phrases, provocative statements, and key facts. I have just given her this speech and asked her to read it to herself a few times.)

Larry: Nyle, which lines in this speech stick out to you? What I mean is, which one or two lines really capture the emotional core of the speech?

Nyle: Well, for me, the lines *"My old house looks so lonesome it tears at my heart"* and *"It has looked lonesome ever since mama died and we moved away"* are the main ones. They are also two of the lines that really got to me when I was choosing the key phrases.

Larry: Nyle, close your eyes and take a deep breath, send the air way down into your belly, and as you let the air out, send yourself the message, "r e l a x...."

(Nyle closes her eyes. She adjusts her back on the chair and uncrosses her legs to get more comfortable. Then, we see her take a deep breath and slowly, she lets the air out.)

Larry: Good, keep your eyes closed. Now, take another breath and this time, as you breathe out, make a sound with that breath.

(Nyle breathes in and this time, as she breathes out, she lets out a very quiet, "aaaahhhhh.")

Larry: Good Nyle, now stay right there with your eyes closed. In this relaxed place, I want you to simply say these words to yourself, "My old house looks so lonesome it tears at my heart it has looked lonesome ever since mama died and we moved away." Say those words quietly to yourself a few times.

(We watch as Nyle says the words to herself. Soon, we see tears running down Nyle's face.)

Larry: Nyle, would you open your eyes and talk with me? *(Nyle opens her eyes, wiping her wet cheek with the back of her right hand.)* What are you experiencing right now?

Nyle: I feel so sad and alone. *(She starts to cry again.)*

Larry: Can you tell me more about that?

Nyle: I think about that house and the rooms inside and how there was once noise and life and now there is nothing, emptiness and it's all so quiet, no voices of children playing together and running in the halls and no parents talking late at night when they think we are asleep but we are listening on the stairs, it's all gone and over and dead and I miss my life in that house and I miss... *(She can't speak.)*

Larry: Who do you miss Nyle?

Nyle: *(After a moment, Nyle looks up.)* Huh?

Larry: Who do you miss right now?

Nyle: Oh God, (*She cries.*) I miss my family and I miss my room and I miss being young and feeling safe.

Larry: Who do you miss the most?

Nyle: Who do I miss most? I miss my little sister, I feel like I've abandoned her, moving to New York and I feel like I made my acting more important than her and she's so much younger than me and she can't understand why I would leave her and now I can never go back, I can never get it back, it will never be the same, I want to be a kid again and I want her to be a baby so I can dress her and take care of her for mom... (*Nyle puts her face into her hand and weeps.*) I miss my mom... I miss my mom... she's my best friend and we talk on the phone but it's not the same and I'm really her main support and I'm not really there for her now, not how I want to be and I know how lonely she really is and how she tries to put up a brave front but... I just want to hold her... I want to hold her...

Larry: Nyle...

Nyle: Yes...

Larry: Say the words, "My old house looks so lonesome it tears at my heart it has looked lonesome ever since mama died and we moved away."

Nyle: (*Looking up to Larry, she is still crying.*) My old house looks so lonesome... it... My old house looks so lonesome it tears... (*Nyle has a hard time getting these words out but she does so very slowly...*) it tears at my heart... it has looked so lonesome ever since my mama died and we moved away... (*Nyle, the tears subsiding, sits very still, looking down at her clasped hands...*)

Larry: All right, Nyle, good. That's enough for now.

Nyle: (*Very quietly, unaware of the mascara running down her face.*) All right.

Larry: Would you like to go to the bathroom and wash some of that makeup from your face?

Nyle: Oh... yeah, that would be good.

Larry: Go ahead, Nyle, take your time. (*Larry turns to the class.*) Let's wait for Nyle. (*Larry and the class wait quietly. After a couple of minutes, Nyle returns and sits down again in the wooden chair. Larry speaks to the class.*) I want you to tell me about your experience out here, as Nyle just spoke Wilma's words from the script?

Miryame: (*Wiping her eyes with a tissue.*) Oh, Larry, I was so moved and heartbroken and when she had trouble saying those words, "it tears at my heart," I just lost it and I wanted to run up there and hug her.... I still do.

Larry: Anyone else?

Francisco: Well, I was also blown away by the power of those words and from how deep down in Nyle they came.

Larry: Tell me more about that part, Francisco, about "from how deep down in Nyle they came."

Francisco: (*He talks rapidly.*) It was really something to watch Nyle talk about the children playing and the house and then, somehow, it all turned into being about her own family and you asked her who she missed the most, and she connected with the meaning her little sister and her mom have to her and how she misses her life with them.

Larry: And what about the words from the play?

Kelly: Yeah, that was really great because Nyle was going through all this very intense stuff about her sister and mom and you asked her to say the words from the play and when she said those words, they were so meaningful and alive and though she was talking about the house and her mama, I know that what was living inside Nyle in that moment was the loss of the life she had with her own mom and her little sister.

Larry: Very good, that's it exactly. And that's what I said earlier about the audience getting two things at the same time — they get the story they hear in the words of the play and they get the "unseen, unstated" story that lives within those words, that lives within all of the actor's behavior, and that comes from the actor's personal investment. Of course, as classmates of Nyle, we were able to witness her own "rehearsal process" and, as privileged insiders, we know something about that "unseen" story. But the audience at the performance of a play does not share in this information, and, the truth is, it's none of their business. It's nobody's business but your own. As Sandy told us, *"If someone should ask you, 'How did you arrive at that incredible meaning you brought to that moment in the play?' Your answer is, 'Talent.'"*

(*Larry turns back to Nyle.*) Nyle, obviously, what you just explored was extremely meaningful to you. And what I want you to do now is come up with a preparation based on that meaning.

Nyle: Could you be more specific?

Larry: Yes. I know you and everyone else here knows that, in terms of activities, preparations, and in all aspects of this Meisner process, we always work from our imagination based on an element of truth. The "element of truth" is the thing that has true meaning to you. So, we start with the element of truth and then, from that foundation, we create imaginary circumstances that are extremely meaningful and very specific.

What you discovered, Nyle, in the work we just did together, was a wonderful element of truth to use in personalizing the emotional core of what Wilma is going through. I'm talking about all the meaning that your little sister and your mom have to you right now in your life. Now, I want you to take that element of truth and use it to build a preparation, which means taking it into the world of your actor's imagination. That makes sense, right?

Nyle: Yeah. You mean coming up with imaginary circumstances that are in the extreme and specific based on the meaning my mom and little sister have to me.

Larry: Right. Also, as you did organically when we worked on the speech, the circumstances must be in line with the emotional essence of the speech. In this case, we are dealing with Wilma's profound sense of loss and needing to care for something that is so important to her.

Nyle: That's clear to me.

Larry: Good. The other part of this is, once you are prepared, then, in talking out loud with your scene partner, you must explore and discover elements in your own "story" that relate to elements in Wilma's "story." In other words, the circumstances you begin to deal with personally must be analogous to those Wilma is dealing with.

(*Larry, in dramatic fashion, suddenly jumps to his feet, does a few Fosse style jazz moves, spins around on his toes, leaps a few feet forward landing on both feet and yells out...*)

Stop!

(*Nyle laughs out loud and the class joins her...*)

Larry: I bet I just confused you all.

(*Larry walks slowly and stares down each of the students, very suspiciously... They continue to laugh...*)

Larry: Yes, I see that I confused every, last, one of you!

(*Larry reverts to his usual suave, debonair, yet, intensely penetrating and enthralling teaching style.*)

Larry: This really isn't complicated and you will discover these things as you work with your acting partner, but let me explain further. (*Larry turns back to Nyle.*) In Wilma's speech, she is dealing with some things that have meaning to her: with the swing, with all the trees, with going away to Hollywood, with the house, and with the loss of her mama. I am saying that, ultimately, you will be creating a personally meaningful "story" that relates in a parallel fashion to Wilma's story. And here's how you will do this Nyle,

1. Spend a lot of time reading the speech to yourself. Get very familiar with the words but don't really memorize them yet.

2. Once you have the preparation figured out and you are very familiar with the speech, you will get together with Miryame and work on the speech. (*Miryame is playing Arabella in the scene.*)

3. Sit across from each other and then, Nyle, turn your back to Miryame and prepare.

4. When you are fully prepared, turn to Miryame and, allowing yourself to ride on the wave of "life" the preparation has induced in you, try to tell her what has happened. (Your imaginary circumstances.) Just say a little bit and then,

5. Still riding on that same wave of life, switch over to Wilma's speech and say some of Wilma's words to Miryame. You don't have to say Wilma's exact words. Since you will be very familiar with the speech, say it as best you know it.

6. Then, go back and improvise more of your own story and then, once again,

7. Go back to Wilma's speech, all the time riding on the preparation.

8. Continue in this manner – improvising your own story, switching to Wilma's words, improvising your own story, switching to Wilma's words – until you have reached the end of the speech. Again, you do all of this after first doing a full preparation.

9. And, Miryame, your job is to listen to Nyle. Sound like fun?

Miryame: (*She giggles.*) Yes, it does.

Larry: Got that, Nyle?

Nyle: Yes, I understand. (*Scrunching up her mouth.*) Now, I just gotta do it.

Larry: Right. Get to work on it. Everyone clear?

(*Braeson leaps to his feet and does his own wild little dance, bounding across the room, singing out in grand southern style, "I AM CLEAR! I AM CLEAR! I AM CLEAR!!" The class is in hysterics. Then Steffi raises her hand waving to Larry.*)

Larry: (*Still laughing...*) Yes, Steffi, do you want to dance too?

Steffi: (*Chuckling...*) Well, no, not at the moment. I just want to make sure I've got this right. So we are actually speaking out our preparation and then we speak the words of the script, back and forth, back and forth?

Larry: Yes, you are kicked off by the preparation. Then, the telling of your own story, becomes an improvisation that will be influenced by the elements of Wilma's speech. Finally, you will have a very meaningful set of imaginary circumstances that, in their own specific way, run parallel with Wilma's circumstances. And, eventually, by working in this back and forth manner, you will infuse Wilma's words with life. Whose life? Your life!

Talea: Larry, this is very exciting. It's really a whole new way of approaching text. Just from seeing even the beginnings of it, in the work that I saw Nyle do, I am so excited.

Larry: It is exciting. And, the great thing is, when you put some real time into actually doing it, the personal meaning you have been working with becomes an intrinsic part of the words. When you reach that point, you don't have to "try" to make your lines meaningful any longer, you see?

What I am talking about is no effort! Simply by you speaking the words and getting out of the way, true life will rise up and express itself through you, on it's own. On its own! And you get to go for the ride of your life with your partners on stage. Only in this way, do you receive the gifts of discovery after discovery, layer beneath layer beneath layer of new possibilities night after night after night: discoveries about this person you are playing and the world he or she lives in; *discoveries that are only possible* when you are not only living truthfully on stage, but *when what you are doing on stage is witnessed* by the other fundamental component of live theater – the audience.

I'm going to make a big deal about this too:

Discoveries are only possible when what you are doing on stage is witnessed by the audience.

Why make a big deal about it? Because most actors think that by the time the play opens, they know it all, and their job is to do their best to repeat what they did in rehearsal or what made the audience laugh last Thursday night. In other words, for these actors, the play is now dead. Sad, you know? Sad to see so many actors sleepwalking their way through the performance. Especially sad for all the poor people who have spent their time and money getting baby-sitters, finding parking, grabbing a bite before the show, and hoping to have the night of their lives at the theater.

I talk too much, I made myself thirsty. (*Larry picks up his soda water and orange juice mix. Takes a quick gulp. Tangy... Zesty...*) Nyle, get to work on that speech and bring it into class on Wednesday.

(*Flashing forward to Wednesday night, we head back into a very quiet Studio Five. In front of class, Nyle sits in the same, wooden chair. Miryame is sitting across from her.*)

Larry: Nyle, Ready to go?

Nyle: Yes, I'm ready.

Larry: Good. For today, using what you have been discovering in your rehearsals, I'll be guiding you through the process of personalizing the speech. From this experience, you'll be able to do it on your own very effectively. Let's begin.

First, as you have done in rehearsals, I want you to turn your back to Miryame and prepare. When you are fully prepared, turn to Miryame and begin telling her your own story. At some point, I will say, "Go to the words." This is your signal to begin using Wilma's words. Then I will say, "Go to your story," which means to tell Miryame your own circumstances. I will take you back and forth in this manner – your own story, then the words of the script, your own story, then the words of the script – until we have gone through a big chunk of the speech.

Also, when I ask you to "Go to the words," if you lose your place in Wilma's speech, don't worry, I have a copy of the speech in my hands and I will let you know where to pick it up from.

Sometimes, I may ask you to repeat certain lines from the script a few times. Or, I may ask you to repeat parts of your own story a few times. So, whatever I say, you say it too. If I don't jump in and say anything else, you keep going. Got it?

Nyle: Yes, I think I do.

Larry: It will be clearer as we actually do it. Two other things. When I speak, stay with what is happening for you emotionally and simply hear my voice as if my words were thoughts in your head. Also, don't look out at me, stay in contact with Miryame as you continue talking with her.

Go ahead and prepare, Nyle.

(Nyle turns her back and begins preparing. Larry and the class wait, in absolute stillness. Larry turns to you, the reader, and leans in. He whispers very quietly...)

Larry: While we are waiting for Nyle to get prepared, I ask that you pay very close attention to how I will be working with her. I am going to interact with Nyle, with her preparation, and with the parallel story she has come up with in rehearsals at home. I will do this in order to help her personalize the speech in a very specific manner. I want you to remember that this is a rehearsal technique only. The aim of it is to help you get to the place where your own, personal meaning lives within the words of the script. So that, ultimately, you will never have to think about or "drum up" the meaning because it will surface on its own simply by you:

a. Speaking the words of the script.

b. Listening to your partners on stage.

c. Being fully present to what is actually happening each night as you live out the circumstances of the play.

d. Taking action. (Which, again, we will get to in the next chapter.)

Larry: Okay readers, I want you to remain very quiet and stay available to Nyle right now. *(Larry turns back to the front of the room where...)*

(After a few minutes, Nyle lets out a deep sigh and turns to Miryame. Nyle looks very sad.)

Nyle: (*Speaking very softly.*) Mom couldn't tell me on the phone, she just couldn't say the words. She just said that Jenny was in the hospital and I needed to get home. I didn't know how bad it was and when I got here, I was too late. I didn't make it in time. I didn't make it in time. Oh Jenny... my sister, my sister... Oh, God... (*Tears stream down Nyle's face.*)

Larry: Go to the words.

Nyle: I love swinging in my front yard...

Larry: Go to your story.

Nyle: I love being in Jenny's room. I tried to make a little place in my apartment in New York for Jenny when she would come and visit, but there is nothing like being in Jenny's room.

Larry: I love being in Jenny's room.

Nyle: I love being in Jenny's room.

Larry: I love to swing in my front yard.

Nyle: I love to swing in my front yard.

Larry: I love being in Jenny's room.

Nyle: I love being in Jenny's room.

Larry: I love to swing in my front yard.

Nyle: I love to swing in my front yard. Aunt Gert also has a swing in her yard, but it's not the same. Mama and I used to come out here and swing together.

Larry: Go to your story, I love being in Jenny's room...

Nyle: I love being in Jenny's room. We could be in here for hours, I'd do her nails and she'd brush my hair.

Larry: Mama and I used to come out here and swing together.

Nyle: Mama and I used to come out here and swing together.

Larry: I'd do her nails and she'd brush my hair.

Nyle: I'd do her nails and she'd brush my hair.

Larry: Mama and I used to come out here and swing together...

Nyle: Mama and I used to come out here and swing together. Some nights my daddy was out gambling and I would wake up and hear Mama out here swinging away. She'd let me come and sit beside her. We'd swing and swing until four in the morning.

Larry: Go to your story.

Nyle: When my dad was leaving my mom, I'd hear Jenny in here singing to herself and I'd come in and end up spending all night in here. I'd read books to her and we'd get under the blanket and sing songs until real late and then she'd fall asleep next to me and I'd watch her breathe...

Larry: Some nights when daddy was out gambling...

Nyle: Some nights when Daddy was out all night gambling, I'd wake up and hear mama swinging away.

Larry: When my dad was leaving my mom, I'd hear Jenny in here singing to herself.

Nyle: When my dad was leaving my mom, I'd hear Jenny in here singing to herself.

Larry: When Daddy was out all night gambling, I'd wake up and hear mama swinging away...

Nyle: When Daddy was out all night gambling, I'd wake up and hear mama swinging away. Sometimes she'd let me sit beside her and we'd swing until three or four in the morning.

Larry: When my dad was leaving my mom...

Nyle: When my dad was leaving my mom, I'd hear Jenny singing and I'd come in and read books to her and we'd get under the blanket and sing songs and then she'd fall asleep next to me and I'd watch her breathe.

Larry: I'd sit beside her and we'd swing until three or four in the morning.

Nyle: I'd sit beside her and we'd swing until three or four in the morning.

Larry: She'd fall asleep next to me and I'd watch her breathe.

Nyle: She'd fall asleep next to me and I'd watch her breathe.

Larry: I'd sit beside her and we'd swing until three or four in the morning.

Nyle: I'd sit beside her and we'd swing until three or four in the morning.

Larry: She'd fall asleep next to me and I'd watch her breathe.

Nyle: She'd fall asleep next to me and I'd watch her breathe.

Larry: Go to the words, the pear tree looks sickly...

Nyle: The pear tree looks sickly, doesn't it? The fig trees are doing nicely. I was out in the back and the weeds are knee high, but fig trees thrive in the weeds. The freeze must have killed off the banana trees...

Larry: Go to your story.

Nyle: This room looks so empty without Jenny. So empty... All her little bears look so lonely without her. It's so quiet and empty without her and it's killing my mom.

Larry: The pear tree looks sickly, doesn't it.

Nyle: The pear tree looks sickly doesn't it.

Larry: The room is so empty without her.

Nyle: The room is so empty without her.

Larry: The freeze killed off the banana trees.

Nyle: The freeze killed off the banana trees.

Larry: It's so quiet and empty and it's killing my mom.

Nyle: It's so quiet and empty and it's killing my mom.

Larry: Say: It's killing my mom, maybe I won't leave either. Maybe I won't go to Hollywood after all.

Nyle: It's killing my mom, maybe I won't leave either. Maybe I won't go to Hollywood after all.

Larry: Maybe I won't leave either. Maybe I won't go to Hollywood after all...

Nyle: Maybe I won't leave either. Maybe I won't go to Hollywood after all. That just comes to me now.

Larry: Go to your story.

Nyle: Maybe I won't go back to New York, maybe I'll put off my acting and stay with mom for a while. I have to stay here with her, she needs me now and I see her sitting and crying and she looks so sad and alone it kills me inside.

Larry: I won't go to Hollywood.

Nyle: I won't go to Hollywood.

Larry: I'll stay with mom for a while.

Nyle: I'll stay with mom for a while.

Larry: She looks so sad and alone it kills me inside.

Nyle: She looks so sad and alone it kills me inside.

Larry: I won't go to Hollywood...

Nyle: I won't go to Hollywood. That just comes to me now.
You know sometimes my old house looks so lonesome
it tears at my heart.

Larry: She looks so sad and alone it kills me inside.

Nyle: She looks so sad and alone it kills me inside.

Larry: My old house looks so lonesome it tears at my heart.

Nyle: My old house looks so lonesome it tears at my heart.

Larry: She looks so sad and alone it kills me inside.

Nyle: She looks so sad and alone it kills me inside.

Larry: My old house looks so lonesome it tears at my heart.

Nyle: My old house looks so lonesome it tears at my heart...

Larry: (*Larry and Nyle both remain quiet for a few*

moments. *Then Larry speaks.*) All right Nyle, let's stop here for today.

Nyle: (*Sitting still, filled with a profound sadness...*) Yes, okay...

Larry: That was wonderful work, Nyle. And, the work is over for right now, okay? Try not to stay in that emotional place, see if you can let it go for now, alright?

Nyle: Yes, I'm all right. That was a powerful experience, whew!

(*There is an excited buzz in the classroom. Larry turns to the students...*)

Larry: (*Turning to the class.*) I know you are all aching to get to the bathroom and have a quick snack. Take a fifteen minute break and then come back so we can discuss the work I did with Nyle.

(*Darryl, Carolina, Tali, Katelyn, Steve, and most of the other students pick up their snack bags and run out of the room. Lisa and Adam stand and stretch. Steven H. unwraps two giant chocolate chip cookies, bites into one, and offers the other to Josie. Larry turns back to you, the reader...*)

Larry: While the class is on break, I want you to go back and read through the work I just did with Nyle. Read those pages of the book at least one more time. It was a lot to digest and reading it again will help you when we come back from the break to talk about this exercise. Don't worry, when the break is over, I'll call you back into class so that you don't miss any of the discussion.

(We flash-forward fifteen minutes. Larry walks to the doorway of Studio Five and out into the hall where the students are talking, laughing, joking, drinking all sorts of bottled waters, finishing up salads, muffins, ice-cream bars, falafel sandwiches, mugs of lobster bisque, big bowls of pasta with meat sauce, tofu burgers, etc.... Larry calls out to the group, "That's it folks, break is over." Twenty-five, well-fed students run back into the studio. Energized and satisfied, they leap, they frolic, they spring and bounce back into the room. And, as promised, Larry also calls to the readers, "Break is over, come on back to class now.")

Larry: (*Walking back into the studio and to the front of the class.*) That was some great work Nyle did, don't you think? Let's talk about it.

Marcy: That was incredible to watch. I could see how you kept helping Nyle take the words from the script and allow those words to ride on the specific meaning of her own, imaginary circumstances. After the work was over, I had an image of what it was like. It was as if Nyle was "planting" her own, personal meaning inside the "soil" of the words.

Larry: That's a great analogy, Marcy. It's very much like planting seeds. Because, as you do this exercise over and over a number of times, those seeds will take root, grow, and then a beautiful life will blossom. So, in terms of what's next for Nyle, I would ask her to do what she did in class today, at home. Got that Nyle?

Continue doing the process we did today. Always do a full preparation and then work your way through the speech, going back and forth — from the words of the script to your own imaginary circumstances — back and forth, back and forth. Also, you are now ready to work your way through the entire speech.

Then, after doing this a bunch of times, learn the words of the speech accurately. When we come back to class, I will have you do a preparation and then say the speech using only the words from the script. No more back and forth. By this time, the meaning you have been "planting," as Marcy called it, will be living on it's own.

Who else has a question or comment?

Christine: That's a lot of work. When we do a play, or even the scenes we are working on, do we have to do this kind of back and forth personalizing exercise with every line in the play?

Larry: I'm glad you asked that. No, you do not do it with every line of the play. Eventually, as you do this exercise and practice it repeatedly, you will make this way of personalizing text more of a habitual skill. What I mean is, you will know when you need to use it to assist you with making the text your own.

Also, although we are doing this process out loud and with a partner, down the road, you will find that you are able to do it more internally and on your own. When you are in a play, the personalizing you do, is part of your homework. Then, when you are in rehearsals with the other actors in the play, you can further integrate the work you did at home. Again, this work "in the mix" with the other actors will be internal. It's like you are becoming accustomed to "seeing" your acting partners through the specific point of view of the character; the point of view that you have been establishing in your own personalizing work at home. (Key phrases, key facts, etc....)

By the way, don't ever come to rehearsal without having done your homework. If you don't have new things to bring to this day's rehearsal, then you are not prepared to work.

Steven H.: That's all related to what I was going to ask, which is, what if I am in a play and the other actors aren't into doing anything like this kind of rehearsal process with me?

Larry: You are right. Most of the time, other actors won't work with you in these ways. Or, the director won't have the interest. Most directors will simply give you the results they want to see and little or no help in arriving at those results. That's why it's important to me that I help you become very strong on your own two feet. Because, most of the time, you will have to do the real work on your own. Sad but true.

Frank: What if there isn't the time to do this kind of work on the script.

Larry: You make the time. That's your job. Also, the more you do this work, the more agile you become in personalizing text so that it doesn't take as much time.

Deborah: What if the circumstances of the speech are very

close to the reality of my own life, do I still need to use different circumstances than in the play to personalize the speech?

Larry: Great question! Of course, the answer is a very individual matter. My own bias is that you must always use your own, invented circumstances, based on the "element of truth" you have chosen to work with. Even if the circumstances you choose are very close to those in the play, you need your own circumstances to make the meaning specifically alive for yourself. Remember, that's the magic word. SPECIFICITY!

Steve H.: This work looks exhausting, does it get easier?

Larry: Well, it's always hard work. But, for me, (as I hope it will be for all of you), this work is an incredible blast. I love the investigation part of the process. I love the work I get to do on the script at home, and I love the work I get to do with the other actors and the director in rehearsals. To me, this is fun! I'm not saying it isn't difficult, painful, frustrating, incredibly challenging, and torture. At times, it's all of those things too. But even when I am in the middle of the darkest despair during rehearsals, somewhere in me, I know I am having the time of my life! I believe, if you are going to stick around and continue doing this thing, you simply have to have fun — or why bother?

Class dismissed for today, see you all next time.

The shortest answer is doing.
English Proverb

chapter eight

taking action

Almost every actor, in every acting class around the country, learns how to "play an action." And, in many acting classes, playing an action or "pursuing your objective" is the primary focus. This results in the creation of, what I call, "objective actors" — actors who have intellectually chosen to "play an action," but who have no real idea why they are playing it! I am saying that,

They do not really know why they are doing what they are doing!

And listen, there are some very facile objective actors. They guilefully move themselves from one action, to the next, to the next, as if the play were one of those connect-the-dots pictures in a child's coloring book. And boy, do they attack those actions with energy! *Yet the words they speak are hollow and their actions are false.* If I haven't said these two great comments from Sandy, I'll say them again,

It's not about showing, it's about knowing.
It's not about being bigger, it's about going deeper.

Another crucial thing I need to let you know is that, for the "objective actor," because he doesn't really know why he is doing what he is doing, there is no true connection to the other actors on stage. Why in the world would it really matter to him how they respond? It doesn't matter to him. Do you see that? This is very important! If he doesn't truly care about why he is doing what he is doing in each moment, how could he possibly really care what the effect of his actions are on his acting partners. He could care less. You see, he's much too busy "playing his actions" to notice what's really going on with the other people on stage. And because he's not personally engaged with what he is doing or "why," — rather than being where he needs to be, (with the other actors and with everything in his environment,) his attention is where it mustn't be (on himself and what a great actor he is).

So, you see, it's with good reason I have saved the lessons in this chapter for last. Up until now, you have been rigorously working on making sure that when you speak the words of the play, you know what you are talking about. Now, you must deal with *WHY* the speaking of those words is necessary. Rather than "action," or "objective," I happen to call this acting element, your *doing*.

Again, for me, the words *action* and *objective* are too cold and technical. Doing, on the other hand, feels much more human. But you know what? I don't care if you call it "Seymour"! What's important is that you do it.

I want you to know that doings are not new to you. If you did the exercises in my previous workbooks, you first learned how to "really do something" in the "activity" assignments that we worked through in Workbook One. In these exercises, the activities not only had to be deeply meaningful to you, they also had to have a tremendous physical difficulty for you. The work on these activities demanded you to reach within yourself and to work with personal meaning; this work trained your concentration, and it strengthened your ability to do something with a one hundred percent commitment – even when what you had to do seemed impossible to achieve!

Then, in Workbook Two, the activities, although still physical in nature, had more of an emotional difficulty. This heightened emotional component intensified your inner struggle to accomplish something that was crucial to you.

Now, I want you to know that, *the "activity," is "every word out of your mouth."*

I am saying that, as an actor, in every moment on stage, you must be involved in something you are doing, something you are trying to accomplish, something you are relentlessly fighting to achieve and that you commit yourself to fully.

And, you must not only know what you are doing, you must also know why you are doing it. Of course, we are talking about the kind of "knowing" we have been working on in every chapter of this book: a knowing "why you are doing what you are doing" that springs from you and your life and that is inspired by the character and the text of the play.

There is another way in which doings are not foreign to you. Simply, as human beings, you and I are continually involved in something we are doing, trying to accomplish, wanting to have happen or need to achieve. If you take an honest look at all of your interactions with the people in your lives, you see that, although mostly unstated and living beneath all of your behavior, there is something specific you are involved in doing. When you become aware of this powerful undercurrent, you realize that your behavior and words are always purposeful. (The next time you go to make a telephone call, right before you punch in the numbers, ask yourself, "Why am I making this call. What am I hoping to achieve? Is it to 'console my sister,' to 'offer an apology,' to 'nurture a friendship'?" What, specifically, do you hope will have happened by the time you hang up?)

Now, to say that all of our words and behavior is purposeful is not to say that we are always "on purpose." What I mean is that, when we look at the things we have done in our lives, it is clear that we do not always act in alignment with our true purpose in life, with our "deeper wish." (Remember "deeper wish" from our conversation on "spine"?) We also realize, that when we take actions that go against our deeper wish, we have to pay the price in one way or another. The same is true for every character, in every play. With every word, with every action and with every ounce of behavior, the character is trying to accomplish that which will get him closer to the fulfillment of his deeply held desires. And, as you and I, he will sometimes do things that sabotage that pursuit. When this happens, he too will pay the price and have to make a mighty effort to rediscover a path that will lead him to the attainment of his deeper wish.

In life, their are many extreme examples of this. Look at the numerous, sickening incidents, of the highly spiritual minister, who, on one hand, is making huge contributions to the lives of his congregation members, and, on the other hand, is sexually abusing one of the children who sings in the choir. (How many stories have become public about television ministers in similar situations?) Or, the brilliant psychotherapist who is helping many of his patients heal from devastating emotional wounds while, at the same time, is using his position of power to abuse some of the women who are in his care. Like I said, these are the extreme examples. Other examples include the guy who suddenly takes the family savings and loses it in a risky stock trade or the rising young executive who steals computer software from her company supply room, as a result of which, she gets fired. Can you think of any examples?

So, everything we do in life, whether it is helping us or hurting us, must be related to our deeper wish. The same for the character in the play. And, just as we have been learning to personalize various aspects of Wilma's life, and learning to personalize the words from the script, I will soon teach you a way to personalize the doings. But before we can get to that...

We are born to action; and whatever is capable of suggesting and guiding action has power over us from the first.
Charles Horton Cooley

chapter   nine

the spine phrase

As I said, we are not yet ready to move on to the doings. First, we need to grapple a little more with the acting element I have just reintroduced, the deeper wish or, the "spine." Let's review our previous discussion:

Every well written character has a profound hunger that shapes the things they say, the things they do, how they respond to the people around them, and to the environment created by the circumstances of the play. It is vital then that we come to terms with the specific nature of the character's desire. We call this aspect of the character, "the spine." When we have a true connection to the character's "spine," we have something to measure the quality of our life on stage, how near or far we are from fulfilling our "deeper wish" in each moment. There it is, my favorite definition of "spine" — the "deeper wish." I love that phrase

172

because first, it has the implication of how utterly private and personal this desire is, and second, it is absolutely active and inherently leads to action.

This is crucial. The spine is not only the character's specific desires, it is also his or her "active response" to that deeper wish.

Do you remember when I asked you to try and come up with a "spine phrase" for yourself? Now it's time to make one for Wilma. To do this, I want to define, more specifically, the key ingredients of the spine phrase. First, let me list these ingredients:

- The spine phrase must be the "bottom line" of the deeper wish.

- The spine phrase must be pointed outward toward the world.

- The spine phrase must be "global" in nature.

- The spine phrase must always be stated as a positive, never as a negative.

- The spine phrase must be stated in an active way.

- The spine phrase must be made of words that are provocative to you personally.

In order to explain these "key ingredients" to you, I will give you a couple of examples of spine phrases for Wilma. As best you can, use the ingredients above and tell me why these are not good spine phrases for Wilma.

Here is one example of a spine phrase for Wilma:

"To keep that house for me"

On the following lines, tell me why this is not a good spine phrase:_____

_____

_____

_____

_____

_____

_____

_____

_____

_____

_____

Let's talk:

First of all, in coming up with a spine phrase, where do we go for inspiration? Yes, of course, we go back to the script and, especially, to the key phrases and the provocative statements that we have already extracted from the script. Let us look together at the first sample spine phrase:

The spine phrase must be the "bottom line" of the deeper wish.

Clearly, "To keep that house for me," is not the "bottom line" of Wilma's deeper wish. Certainly, Wilma does not want to lose the house. But we know that the house, as a physical structure, is the outer layer of more deeply seated issues. There is Wilma's remaining connections to her mother and to a time when life was warm and safe, there is Wilma's longing to be close with her father and to be a part of her true family, there are Wilma's hopes for her future as an adult and having a family of her own in the house, and there is the powerful pull of Harrison itself and Wilma's passion to live in her house, in this town, that is the bread and wine of Wilma's soul.

The spine phrase must be pointed outward toward the world.

Do you see how the phrase, "To keep that house for me," rather than being pointed out toward the world, is pointed back at Wilma herself? By making the spine phrase point out to the world, the phrase will help you inhabit a point of view that connects with all of the other people in Wilma's world.

The spine phrase must be "global" in nature.

By "global," I mean that the spine phrase must be stated in such a way that it can include all of the things Wilma is involved in doing in her life (what she is doing in the play and what we imagine she does when we don't see her in the play), as well as all of the people she encounters in her life (not only the people we meet in the play, but all of the people Wilma relates to who are not in the play). This incites our imagination — how does Wilma go about fulfilling her deeper wish in other situations and circumstances? For instance, how does she behave when she is at school with her other friends and with her teachers?

Here is another possible spine phrase:

"To be mean and rotten to old lady Leighton"

On the following lines, tell me why this is not a good spine phrase:_____

_____

_____

_____

_____

_____

_____

_____

_____

_____

Again, *"To be mean and rotten to old lady Leighton"* is not the bottom line of Wilma's deeper wish. And, although this time the phrase is not directed at Wilma herself, it is still too narrow and confined, meaning, it is not "global" in its scope. If you chose this as a spine phrase, it would result in some behavior toward Mrs. Leighton, but how could it possibly help you (as Wilma) relate to Minna, or Arabella, or the shorthand teacher, or Jay Godfrey, or anyone else? It couldn't.

The other reason I gave you this phrase as an example is the following item from our list of ingredients:

The spine phrase must always be stated as a positive, never as a negative.

No character considers the things they do in a negative light. For every character, his or her actions are justified, warranted, and rightful. So, it is very important that the deeper wish be stated in a way that helps you feel good about what you are trying to achieve.

Two ingredients from our list I haven't mentioned yet are, first: *The spine phrase must be stated in an active way.*

Simply, the phrase must help lead you to doing something. So, if you were playing a part and you came up with "To wonder if my life's going in the right direction" as a spine phrase, I would have to tell you that you have not made a good choice. How would "to wonder" lead you into taking action? It wouldn't. It would basically lead you to sitting around and, generally, thinking things over.

And, the final ingredient I listed: The spine phrase must be made of words which are provocative to you personally.

This makes sense, doesn't it? I mean, if you are the one who is going to choose the words, why not choose words that are juicy to you, that stimulate you? This isn't just good advice, this is essential. The words must resonate in you, in a way that stirs your soul, arouses your imagination, and, when stated in an active way, compels you to take action.

So, what might a good spine phrase for Wilma be? Well, here's an example that has some interesting possibilities. Let's try it on for size: *"To keep the family alive."*

First of all, for me, these words are provocative. The words "To keep the family alive" do something to me personally. And with Wilma's circumstances brewing in me, from all the work I have been doing with the script, these words really get my insides stirring. Also, these words make me want to take action — "I must not allow any harm to come to the loved ones in my life or to those things in my world that protect them." Aren't these Wilma's fundamental concerns?

There is the devastating loss at a young age of her mama. Now, Wilma even struggles with the difficulty of holding her mama's image in her mind. Can't you imagine her sitting in bed at night, looking at her mama's picture and trying to retain every detail? Wouldn't this be an activity necessitated by Wilma's need "to keep the family alive"?

There has been a great chasm in her relationship with her daddy, who, after all, was the one who broke her mama's heart. But Wilma comes to forgive her daddy, and we hear her confide in Arabella of her powerful love for him. Isn't this forgiveness and love an outcome of Wilma's deep seated desire "To keep the family alive"?

Wilma is now threatened with another kind of "death," the fear of losing her daddy, which is caused by the impending marriage of her daddy to Mrs. Leighton. Can you see how Wilma's tough attitudes toward Mrs. Leighton would come from Wilma's determination "To keep the family alive"?

There is, of course, the house and all that it represents for Wilma. Isn't it absolutely clear that Wilma's love for the house, her continual need to go to the house, and her tenaciousness in not allowing it to be taken away from her, is all a result of her hunger "To keep the family alive."

Toward the end of the play, Wilma and Mrs. Leighton make a wonderful, new connection. And because of Mrs. Leighton, Wilma and her daddy also have a beautiful reawakening of their love for each other. Out of this event, Wilma experiences a deep-rooted sense of joy and excitement. She is thrilled: to be invited by Mrs. Leighton to call her "Sibyl," to be invited to the wedding, and to be invited to stay with her daddy and Sybil for the summer in Houston! Doesn't Wilma's core-level jubilation come from her surprising triumph in "keeping the family alive"?

Going back to our list of ingredients for the spine phrase, I would say that "To keep the family alive" is the bottom line of Wilma's deeper wish. It is a phrase that is also pointed out toward the world and is global in nature. We can see how "keeping the family alive" influences her conversations and activities with Minna, with Aunt Gert, with Arabella (going to the house together, asking if Arabella remembers her mama...), and we can imagine how it reveals itself in other relationships that are not defined in the play. I would certainly say that the word *family* is one of the most important words in the English language for Wilma. Wouldn't you?

Now it's your turn. Go back to your key phrases and provocative statements and come up with a spine phrase for Wilma with words that do something way down in you. When you have a phrase, write it on the following line:

Spine Phrase:_____

_____

If you have come up with your own spine phrase for Wilma, you may move on to the next chapter in the book.

Talk that does not end in any kind of action
is better suppressed altogether.
Thomas Carlyle

c h a p t e r   t e n

doing

With our spine phrase established, we are better prepared to uncover what Wilma is involved in doing in each moment because we can now ask ourselves, "How does this relate to my deeper wish"? The important thing to note here is that you cannot act the spine. I'll say that in another way. You do not act the spine directly. It is the spine, the deeper wish, that makes everything you do on stage essential. So, having the spine phrase will help you stay on course in relationship to, one, what is really "driving" Wilma, and two, how this manifests itself in the actions Wilma takes. Remember, everything Wilma is involved in must be seen through the specific "lens" of the spine phrase.

Here's an interesting puzzle. As I start to look at doings and think about the beginning of the play, I have to wonder, how does going to Hollywood and becoming a movie star relate to the spine phrase I came up with, "To keep the family alive"? At first it might not seem to fit. But having strong feelings about the power of this particular phrase, I must investigate further. First, I know from the play that Wilma certainly fantasizes about what she can do for her loved ones if she becomes famous and successful. Here's something she says to Minna:

WILMA. Oh, Minna. I love you. And you know what I'm going to do? I'm going to be a great movie star and send my chauffeur and my limousine to Harrison and put you in it and drive you all the way to Hollywood.

But there is an even more intriguing question for me. Let's imagine that Arabella wants to go to Houston for the screen test with Mr. Delafonte, as much as Wilma does. And, when Wilma opens her letter on the swing, reads the good news, and says to Arabella, "Well, let's pack our bags. Hollywood, here we come," let's imagine that Arabella says, "Yippee, let's go!" Then, let's suppose that the girls each tiptoe into their rooms, pack a bag with clothes, and make it to the train station without the parents, Aunt Gert, or Minna finding out. The question I must ask is, do I think Wilma would actually get on that train and go? Knowing what I know about how she truly feels about her life in Harrison, about the house, about her mama and about her daddy, would she really follow through on her fantasy of becoming a movie star? I'm not going to answer that question because I want you to give it some thought. Do you think she would go? All I will say, after considering this myself, is that I still believe my spine phrase is a valid one.

All right. In order to talk about doings, we are going to

use the following little chunk of the play. Read through it one time:

MAN. I beg your pardon. Is this the Thompson house?

(*They stop swinging.*)

WILMA. Yes sir.

MAN. I understand it's for sale. I'd like to look around.

WILMA. No sir. It's not for sale. It's for rent. I'm Wilma Thompson. I own the house. My daddy rents it for me...

MAN. Oh, well, we were told by Mr. Mavis...

WILMA. I'm sure. Mr. Mavis tries to sell everything around here. He's pulled that once before about our house, but this house is not for sale. It's for rent.

MAN. You're sure?

WILMA. I'm positive. We rent it for twenty-seven fifty a month. You pay lights, water, and keep the yard clean. We are very particular over how the yard is kept. I'd be glad to show it to you...

MAN. I'm sorry. I was interested in buying. There must have been a mistake.

WILMA. There must have been.

MAN. Where could I find your father, young lady?

WILMA. Why do you want to see him?

MAN. Well, I'd just like to get this straight. I understood from Mr. Mavis...

WILMA. Mr. Mavis has nothing to do with my house. My house is for rent, not for sale.

MAN. All right. (*The MAN leaves. He goes out r. c. of the yard area.*)

WILMA. The nerve of old man Mavis putting out around town that my house is for sale. Isn't that nervy, Arabella?

(*ARABELLA gets out of the swing.*)

ARABELLA. We'd better go. It'll be dark soon. The tree frogs are starting.

WILMA. It just makes me furious. Wouldn't it make you furious?

ARABELLA. Come on. Let's go.

WILMA. Wouldn't it make you furious?

ARABELLA. Yes.

WILMA. You don't sound like you mean it.

ARABELLA. Well...

WILMA. Well... What?...

ARABELLA. Nothing... Let's go.

WILMA. Arabella, you know something you're not telling me.

ARABELLA. No, I don't. Honest, Wilma...

WILMA. You do. Look at me, Arabella...

ARABELLA. I don't know anything. I swear...

WILMA. You do. I thought you were my friend.

ARABELLA. I am. I am.

WILMA. Well, then why don't you tell me?

ARABELLA. Because I promised not to.

WILMA. Why?

ARABELLA. Well... I...

WILMA. What is it? Arabella, please tell me.

ARABELLA. Well... Will you never say I told you?

WILMA. I swear.

ARABELLA. Well, I didn't tell you before because in all the excitement in telling you I wasn't going to Hollywood and your saying you weren't going, I forgot about it... until that man came...

WILMA. What is it, Arabella? What is it?

ARABELLA. Well, I heard my daddy tell my mother that Mr. Lester had taken out a license to marry Mrs. Leighton.

WILMA. Oh, well. That doesn't surprise me too much. I've been looking for that to happen.

ARABELLA. But that isn't all, Wilma...

WILMA. What else?

ARABELLA. Well...

WILMA. What else?

ARABELLA. Well...

WILMA. What else, Arabella? What else?...

ARABELLA. Well... My daddy heard that your daddy had put this house up for sale...

WILMA. I don't believe you...

ARABELLA. That's what he said, Wilma... I... He said Mr. Lester came to him and wanted to know if he wanted to buy it...

WILMA. Well. He won't do it. Not my house. He won't do it! (*WILMA has jumped out of the swing and runs out of the yard u. c.*)

ARABELLA. Wilma... Wilma... Please... don't say I said it... Wilma...

Now, the first thing we need to talk about is breaking the scene down into "beats." Have you heard this word used in relation to acting, "beat"? It is a widely used acting term and, simply, it means "a unit of action." So, within a beat, a character has one, primary thing he or she is trying to achieve. When that which the character is fighting to accomplish changes, we have a new beat. Using beats is a very helpful tool in getting absolutely specific about what it is you are doing in each moment of the play. Because, if I were your director, and I were to stop and ask you, "What are you doing right now, what are you after here in this moment?," you must be able to answer me in a specific way.

The play is like a river, but we can't possibly experience the entire river at one time. As you travel along a river, you are continually flowing into new landscapes — yet — all parts of the river relate organically to the whole. The play too has an organic through-line, as does the character. But you cannot act the through-line. It's too big. Any attempt to do so would result in a completely general approach to the part. And, as you know from previous lessons, anything left general in your approach will result in your acting being general. What do I mean by "general"? Hazy, mushy and vague! (Not good words for actors.) So, the play must be broken down into act-able portions, each portion flowing into the next, and all portions related to the whole.

Right now, I want you to go back to the little scene I just gave to you with Wilma, Arabella, and the Man. See if you can figure out, for Wilma, what the beats are. To do that, keep asking yourself, "What is Wilma trying to make happen"? or "What does Wilma want to give to, or get from, the other person"? When you have an idea of what

Wilma is trying to accomplish, see how long she continues in that effort. When she stops doing one thing and begins to do something else, that's a new beat. Give it a try. You do it first and then I will show you what I came up with.

. . .

Here's how I broke this part of the play into beats:

BEAT ONE

MAN. I beg your pardon. Is this the Thompson house?

(*They stop swinging.*)

WILMA. Yes sir.

MAN. I understand it's for sale. I'd like to look around.

BEAT TWO

WILMA. No sir. It's not for sale. It's for rent. I'm Wilma
    Thompson. I own the house. My daddy rents it for me...

MAN. Oh, well, we were told by Mr. Mavis...

WILMA. I'm sure. Mr. Mavis tries to sell everything around
    here. He's pulled that once before about our house, but
    this house is not for sale. It's for rent.

MAN. You're sure?

WILMA. I'm positive. We rent it for twenty-seven fifty a month. You pay lights, water, and keep the yard clean. We are very particular over how the yard is kept. I'd be glad to show it to you...

MAN. I'm sorry. I was interested in buying. There must have been a mistake.

WILMA. There must have been.

MAN. Where could I find your father, young lady?

WILMA. Why do you want to see him?

MAN. Well, I'd just like to get this straight. I understood from Mr. Mavis...

WILMA. Mr. Mavis has nothing to do with my house. My house is for rent, not for sale.

MAN. All right. (*The MAN leaves. He goes out r. c. of the yard area.*)

BEAT THREE

WILMA. The nerve of old man Mavis putting out around town that my house is for sale. Isn't that nervy, Arabella?

(*ARABELLA gets out of the swing.*)

ARABELLA. We'd better go. It'll be dark soon. The tree frogs are starting.

WILMA. It just makes me furious. Wouldn't it make you furious?

ARABELLA. Come on. Let's go.

WILMA. Wouldn't it make you furious?

ARABELLA. Yes.

WILMA. You don't sound like you mean it.

ARABELLA. Well...

WILMA. Well... What?...

ARABELLA. Nothing... Let's go.

BEAT FOUR

WILMA. Arabella, you know something you're not telling me.

ARABELLA. No, I don't. Honest, Wilma...

WILMA. You do. Look at me, Arabella...

ARABELLA. I don't know anything. I swear...

WILMA. You do. I thought you were my friend.

ARABELLA. I am. I am.

WILMA. Well, then why don't you tell me?

ARABELLA. Because I promised not to.

WILMA. Why?

ARABELLA. Well... I...

WILMA. What is it? Arabella, please tell me.

ARABELLA. Well... Will you never say I told you?

WILMA. I swear.

ARABELLA. Well, I didn't tell you before because in all the excitement in telling you I wasn't going to Hollywood and your saying you weren't going, I forgot about it... until that man came...

WILMA. What is it, Arabella? What is it?

ARABELLA. Well, I heard my daddy tell my mother that Mr. Lester had taken out a license to marry Mrs. Leighton.

WILMA. Oh, well. That doesn't surprise me too much. I've been looking for that to happen.

ARABELLA. But that isn't all, Wilma...

WILMA. What else?

ARABELLA. Well...

WILMA. What else?

ARABELLA. Well...

WILMA. What else, Arabella? What else?...

ARABELLA. Well... My daddy heard that your daddy had put this house up for sale...

WILMA. I don't believe you...

ARABELLA. That's what he said, Wilma... I... He said Mr. Lester came to him and wanted to know if he wanted to buy it...

BEAT FIVE

WILMA. Well. He won't do it. Not my house. He won't do it! (*WILMA has jumped out of the swing and runs out of the yard u. c.*)

ARABELLA. Wilma... Wilma... Please... don't say I said it... Wilma...

. . .

As you can see, I broke the scene down into five beats. How many did you get??

Let's move on and talk about the doings.

Again, in each beat, Wilma has one main objective she is pursuing. The way we can arrive at what she is doing is first to read the beat and ask ourselves, "What is Wilma *actually doing?*" What do I mean by "actually" doing? I mean, what is Wilma doing, in a *literal way,* with the other people in each beat. These actual doings may or may not be the doings we will ultimately use to personalize, but it is the first phase of arriving at them.

Here's an example of arriving at the actual doing:

In beat one, we know that before the Man comes into the scene, Wilma and Arabella have just shared a very sweet moment and Wilma has made an important decision for the direction of her life. Then, as Horton tells us,

> (*WILMA gets back in the swing. They swing vigorously back and forth... A MAN comes in r. c. of the yard area.*)

So, in the middle of this happy moment between Wilma and Arabella, a *total stranger* walks in and asks about *Wilma's house*. Now normally, I don't pay much attention to stage directions, and Horton, understanding an actor's true needs, doesn't weigh us down with any unnecessary information or instructions. So, when Horton does give a stage direction, I listen! In this beat, when the Man asks about the house, Horton says,

> (*They stop swinging.*)

Now, just that alone gives me a specific feeling about this moment between the Man and Wilma. But also, as I just said, this Man is a stranger to Wilma and he is inquiring about the most precious thing in her life! Isn't it understandable how, under these circumstances, Wilma would be extremely cautious with this man? I would say, yes, it is understandable. And for me, that would be my "actual" or literal doing. I would say it this way:

To treat him cautiously.

Again, this may not be the doing we will ultimately work with. Why? Well, hold on to that question as we will come back to it very soon. Before we do though, it is your turn to do some work.

Right now, I want you to work with the beats as I have broken them down and look at them closely. Then, as I just did with Beat One, I want you to come up with an actual doing for each beat. As you find them and choose a way to say them, write your actual doings here in the book. After you write the phrase down, write how you arrived at your choices in the "notes" sections. Please do that now:

Beat One: _____

Notes: _____

_____

_____

_____

_____

_____

_____

_____

Beat Two: _____

Notes: _____

_____

_____

_____

_____

_____

_____
_____
_____

Beat Three: _____
Notes: _____
_____
_____
_____
_____
_____
_____
_____
_____

Beat Four: _____
Notes: _____
_____
_____
_____
_____
_____
_____
_____
_____

Beat Five: _____
Notes: _____
_____
_____
_____

_____

_____

_____

_____

. . .

How did that go? Here now, are the actual doings I came up with. (Remember, this may or may not be the way we will ultimately phrase the doings when we begin to work with them with our acting partner.)

Beat One: To treat him cautiously

Beat Two: To make him see his mistake

Beat Three: To win her agreement

Beat Four: To get the information out of her

Beat Five: To fight back

. . .

All right, now we have some initial doings to get us going. But the ultimate test for how well a doing works for you is in the doing of it. You can sit around and come up with fabulous doings or actions from morning until night, but they won't really mean a thing until you discover what it is truly like to actually do them. And do them with whom? Yes, with the other actors. This is where all the early work on being fully available to your partners on stage and on freeing your instinctual responsiveness comes back into play.

You see, the first thing the doing must do is "incite you to action." This is why, the way you say the doing is very important. A good question to ask yourself is, "Do the words I have chosen for the doing make me want to do it"? Also, as with the spine phrase, the way you say the doing must be pointed out toward the other person rather than back at yourself. This will help you become like an arrow, always aimed directly in the direction of what you are trying to achieve.

So, once you have figured out what it is you are doing, what do you think it is that determines how you go about doing it? Great question!

Here's an example. Let's take the doing I gave to Beat Four: "To get the information out of her." And, let's create an imaginary circumstance (unrelated to the play), in which "To get the information out of her" is what you are doing:

Let's say that you, the husband, have come home from work. You come into the kitchen and, taking off your coat, you see the day's mail on the counter. In the pile of mail, you find a credit card bill from American Express and you open it. You look at the statement and discover that your balance is a whopping nine thousand dollars! You know that you didn't use this particular credit card all last month, (you used your Visa card). You look further down and you see the name of some odd-sounding investment company that you never heard of. They got nine thousand dollars of your money! You also know that only two people in this family share this American Express card – you and your wife. Furious, you call out to your wife. No answer. Her car was in the driveway, where is she? Extremely upset, you look in the living room. She's not there. Tense and angrier by the minute, you check the bathrooms. Vacant. You go into the bedroom and you see your wife's long hair sticking out from beneath the blankets on the bed...

This is where you are injected, catapulted, into your doing,

"To get the information out of her!"

Wait... Let's pause right here...

What, do you think, will determine how you go about "getting the information out of her"? Write your thoughts down on the following blank lines:

_____

_____

_____

_____

_____

The answer is, two things determine how you go about "pursuing your objective." And, these two things are interwoven, always working in conjunction with each other. Each is equally important. These two things are:

1. Your true desire

2. What is being conveyed to you by the other person.

What am I telling you is, you are motivated to "do what you do" because of your deeper desires AND, AT THE

SAME TIME, you must continually be in response to what you are getting from your partners. Why? Because, if you are really available to them, it is your partners on stage who will tell you if you are getting *closer to* or *more distant from* fulfilling your needs and wants.

Let's go back to our example.

You are outraged because your wife gave away nine thousand dollars of your hard-earned money to some shady investment company, and she did it behind your back. You have finally found her in the bedroom, under the blankets, and you are going to "get the information out of her!" Suppose, as a first attempt, you hold in your anger. You could easily explode, but you will try to remain calm. Standing near the bed you quietly ask, "I want you to explain this American Express bill to me." There is no response. You try again. "I am waiting for an explanation." This time the blankets move as your wife turns away from you. Obviously, this approach isn't working. With some force, you rip the blankets away and demand, "I need to know where this nine thousand dollars went and I want to know right now!" Suddenly, your wife leaps off of the bed, runs into the bathroom, and locks the door. In a flash, you discover yourself banging on that door, screaming, "Come out of there and tell me what the hell is going on here!" Then, you hear crying from inside the bathroom. Soon, the door is slowly unlocked and, inch by inch, the door opens. Your wife stands there looking at the carpet and sobs. Her moans are so deep that they rip into your heart, and though you still shake with anger, you find you just can't speak. You remain silent for a few moments while your wife cries and then you reach down and take her hand. As you lead her back to the bed, you say, "Come on, come on, let's talk this out. Okay, honey"?

What I have just played out for you is an example of how "your true desire" and "what is being conveyed to you by the other person" are always the interrelated source of how you do what you do. In our story, we can see how the husband, fueled by his rage at his wife's use of the credit card, truly needed to get the story out of her. And from beginning to end, he never gave up that doing. Even when he takes her hand at the end and says, "Come on, come on, let's talk this out. Okay, honey?" he is still working on "getting the information out of her." We also see clearly that, because the wife's behavior changed from moment to moment, the ways in which the husband went about getting the story out of her changed as well. We can say that the husband was continually *"adjusting"* his efforts to get information, as he *"worked off"* the meaning of his wife's behavior. This is so, so vital. I can't say enough about how important this is. So, I will say it again in this way:

> You must be in continual adjustment to your part-
> ners on stage as you are "available to" and "working
> off" the meaning of their behavior.

A few more things pertaining to the way you say the doing. Sometimes the way you have chosen to say the "actual" doing will be good enough to work with, and sometimes, you will have to cut a layer deeper. What you are looking for is to find a way to say the phrase that you feel is the true "core" of what the character is doing. For example, if my actual doing was "giving my wife a mas-sage," my core doing might be "to make her queen for a day!" So, if your "actual" doing doesn't really get to the bottom line of the doing, you will have to dig your way down to the "core." Also, isn't it more fun and provocative to say "to make her queen for a day"!? It certainly is for me.

A couple of other useful things to know when you put together a doing, is that, first, it is helpful to use active verbs. For example: *to implore, to denounce, to warn, to dissuade, to admonish, to discipline, to forbid, to celebrate, to commend, to set right, and so forth.* As I said earlier, the doings must be said in a way that incites you to action and directs you out toward the other people on stage. Active verbs help do this.

What you must not create are phrases that put your attention back on yourself. For example, the kinds of phrases that *will not* help you are phrases like these: *to get disturbed, to be enraged, to be resentful, to be bashful, to be sweet, and so on.* These phrases not only leave your partners on stage out of the picture, they will call on you to produce some conventionalized, clichéd idea of an emotional state. You can not act a state! If you do, all you are really doing is making a "mood." Spell "mood" backwards! What do you get?

Also, if you recall, way back in our early lessons, I taught you that acting is not "emoting," acting is *doing something.* You learned that when you put your attention on doing something, and when the thing you are doing is meaningful to you, your emotions come to life as a gift. As Sandy said, "The quality of your acting depends on how fully you do what you are doing!"

One more thing.

Everything I am telling you here is only good if it helps you. What I am saying is, although I know all of these aspects of doings will assist you nicely, there are times when you will find that something very different will be even more persuasive. What if, in a certain beat, you called your doing, "The lion devours" or in another beat, "Tarzan saves the day!" or, "The egg sizzles!" *Ultimately, if you understand it and it leads you to take action in a specific, personal and meaningful way — Hey! Why not use it?* In the end, no one cares how you get there, as long as you get there. Where's "there"? Bringing a passionate, relentless and pulsating life to the stage!

· · ·

I am now going to show you how to personalize a doing.

Ready?

Let's do some more work on Beat Four:

BEAT FOUR

WILMA. Arabella, you know something you're not telling me.

ARABELLA. No, I don't. Honest, Wilma...

WILMA. You do. Look at me, Arabella...

ARABELLA. I don't know anything. I swear...

WILMA. You do. I thought you were my friend.

ARABELLA. I am. I am.

WILMA. Well, then why don't you tell me?

ARABELLA. Because I promised not to.

WILMA. Why?

ARABELLA. Well... I...

WILMA. What is it? Arabella, please tell me.

ARABELLA. Well... Will you never say I told you?

WILMA. I swear.

ARABELLA. Well, I didn't tell you before because in all the
excitement in telling you I wasn't going to Hollywood
and your saying you weren't going, I forgot about it...
until that man came...

WILMA. What is it, Arabella? What is it?

ARABELLA. Well, I heard my daddy tell my mother that Mr.
Lester had taken out a license to marry Mrs. Leighton.

WILMA. Oh, well. That doesn't surprise me too much. I've
been looking for that to happen.

ARABELLA. But that isn't all, Wilma...

WILMA. What else?

ARABELLA. Well...

WILMA. What else?

ARABELLA. Well...

WILMA. What else, Arabella? What else?...

ARABELLA. Well... My daddy heard that your daddy had put this house up for sale...

WILMA. I don't believe you...

ARABELLA. That's what he said, Wilma... I... He said Mr. Lester came to him and wanted to know if he wanted to buy it...

. . .

Again, I said the actual doing for this beat was:

"To get the information out of her."

Do you think we should work with this phrase, as it is? Does it incite you to take action? Are the words provocative to you? If not, on the following line, write down the way you would like to say the doing for this beat:

The doing is:_____

For me, I would have to find another way, a more provocative way, to phrase the doing. But rather than talk about it, let's go back into class where Nyle and Miryame happen to be working on this very beat. (What a coincidence!) Again, pay close attention. In the following work with Nyle and Miryame, I will teach you the way to personalize the doings....

(We are now back in Studio Five. Nyle and Miryame sit in chairs in front of the class and they are talking with Larry...)

Larry: Nyle, tell me how you phrased the actual doing for Beat Four.

Nyle: Well, now, after what you told us about how to say the phrase in the most act-able way, I see that my actual doing phrase doesn't really turn me on to take action.

Larry: How did you word it?

Nyle: For the "actual doing," I said that Wilma is trying to "to get the information out of her."

Larry: Well, you and I chose the same "actual doing."

Nyle: Yes, I know... Uhh, Larry?

Larry: Yes?

Nyle: I have to admit that I got it from your new Meisner Approach book, in which I appear as a fictitious character.

Larry: Oh, you read the book... Really?

Nyle: Yes, it's wonderful.

Larry: But, Nyle, I am still writing it. How in the world did you...

Nyle: Ummm... I don't really know exactly, but I did enjoy it very much.

Larry: I'm glad.

Nyle: I'm sorry I stole your actual doing for this beat.

Larry: Well, it's fine with me that you used my actual doing because it will help the rest of the fictional characters here in the book, and the readers, see how we can make this particular phrase more provocative for you — make it more appetizing, so that it will, as you said, "turn you on to take action."

Nyle: Good.

Larry: So what are your thoughts about how you want to say it?

Nyle: Well, I know Arabella knows something and that she's scared to tell me, so I know it must be important stuff she's not saying. She denies knowing anything, so it's like she's standing there lying to me and it's crucial that I know what's really going on.

Larry: So what do you want to do about that?

Nyle: I want the truth out of her.

Larry: Well, if you sit around and wait, will she give it to you?

Nyle: No, she won't.

Larry: So what will you do?

Nyle: I will demand that she gives me the truth.

Larry: Now say that as a doing phrase.

Nyle: To demand the truth.

Larry: Yes! Is that something you can do?

Nyle: Yes.

Larry: Is that something you *want and need* to do?

Nyle: Yes it is.

Larry: And *when* do you need to do it?

Nyle: Right now.

Larry: That's right. So, there you are. You have your phrase
   to work with. How about you Miryame.

Miryame: Larry... May I ask something first?

Larry: Of course.

Miryame: Am I... Am I a fictional character too?

Larry: Well... Yes Miryame, yes you are.

Miryame: Oh... Oh, I see... Okay.

Larry: Was that all, Miryame?

Miryame: Yes, that was all.

Larry: And what did you come up with as an actual doing for Arabella in this beat.

Miryame: When I look at the beat literally, I know that I am protecting myself. I'm scared. I mean, Wilma's my best friend and I have news that I know she would want, but I am afraid to tell her because I promised not to tell, and if I do, I will be in big trouble.

Larry: So what is your "actual," or literal, doing?

Miryame: I am protecting myself.

Larry: Now, would you want to use that as your doing to work with?

Miryame. No, and the strongest reason is that it is pointed at myself, and when I think about this phrase, I do not feel like it leads me to take action, specifically, with Wilma.

Larry: Talk it out some more and see if you can find a better way to say it. Let me ask you this, when you read it, how do you feel about Wilma's behavior in this beat?

Miryame: I'm frightened.

Larry: Why?

Miryame: Because she is so forceful and she keeps hammering away at me.

Larry: I like that, "hammering away at you." You know, for anyone else, Wilma's pushing to get information probably wouldn't seem all that fierce. But from Arabella's viewpoint, absolutely, it is! So you feel like Wilma is doing what to you?

Miryame: It's like she's attacking me, like she's all over me.

Larry: Do you want to be attacked in this manner?

Miryame: No, I don't like it a bit. I wish the whole thing never came up so that I wouldn't get into trouble. But now, the cat's out of the bag and I don't want to lose my best friend, but I still don't want to get into trouble...

Larry: What do you *want* to do right now?

Miryame: I want her to back off.

Larry: Well it would be nice if she did. Do you think she's going to leave you alone?

Miryame: No, she won't give up.

Larry: So what *must* you do right now?

Miryame: I must get her to back off.

Larry: Now say it as a doing phrase.

Miryame: To back her off.

Larry: I think that's something you can do. Do you?

Miryame: Yes, I can do that.

Larry: All right, now I will show you how to personalize the doings. Nyle, say what you are doing.

Nyle: I am demanding the truth.

Larry: And you Miryame?

Miryame: I am backing her off.

Larry: I want both of you to take some time right now to create, in your mind, an imaginary circumstance in which you would need and want to do your doing. As always, you must find an imaginary circumstance based on an element of truth.

Let me make this much clearer!

As I have told you before, in acting the part, we must go away from the circumstances of the play because, although the circumstances are specifically meaningful to the characters in the play, they do not have specific meaning to us. So, in order to personalize what we must achieve — what we must strive to accomplish — we have to find a way to make the character's doings, our own.

To do this, you must ask yourselves, "Under what circumstances would I, Nyle, be compelled to "demand the truth"? "Under what circumstances would I, Miryame, be compelled to 'back her off'?"

The answer to the question is:

It is "AS IF" _____

    The blank then, must be filled in with a situation that makes you want and need to do the doing you have chosen to work with.

    For you Nyle, you need to create a situation in which it would be imperative for you to "demand the truth!" from someone. You create this situation out of your imagination, founded on an element of truth. The element of truth is what makes you, Nyle, truly need to get the truth out of the other person. And get the truth when? Right now!

    And for you Miryame, you need an imaginary circumstance in which someone is intensely pressuring you, and if you give in, there will be terrible consequences for you. This compels you to "back that person off!" Is that clear to both of you?

Miryame: Yes, I am clear.

Nyle: It's clear and I have one question. Since I have been working on the scene using imaginary circumstances based on the meaning of my sister and my mother, should I connect this personalizing work to that other stuff?

Larry: Yes, yes, yes yes! Great question! It is a wonderful and important idea to relate and connect, in some way, the meaning here in this work on the doings to the elements of personal meaning you have been working with previously. In this way, you begin to create your own, specific and intimate emotional through-line for the whole play.

Go ahead now, both of you, turn your chairs to face each other, close your eyes and come up with imaginary circumstances that make you need to do the doing. When you are ready, open your eyes and look at each other.

(*Nyle and Miryame stand, turn their chairs, sit back down facing each other and close their eyes. All of us, fictional or not, wait quietly... After a few minutes, Miryame opens her eyes. Moments later, Nyle does also.*)

Larry: I want both of you to look at each other and stay with each other as we go through this. (*Nyle and Miryame look at each other.*) Nyle, in your "as if," who are you talking to? Just give me the first name.

Nyle: I am talking to cousin Edna.

Larry: Miryame, who are you talking to?

Miryame: To my friend Teri.

Larry: Okay. In a moment I am going to ask you, one at a time, to begin talking to the person you just mentioned. Nyle, I will start with you. When I tell you to begin, you will talk to cousin Edna and "demand the truth!" Basically, you will be doing a free association, out loud, that comes out of your imaginary circumstance and is driven by your need "to demand the truth!" Miryame, same thing for you. At some point, I will switch over to you, and I will tell you to talk to Teri and to "back her off."

When I ask each of you to talk, here are the key things I want both of you to do:

- Keep talking, do not stop.
- Attempt not to pause — keep talking.
- If you don't have the words, keep talking.
- Allow yourself to say whatever comes out of your mouth.
- Do not censor anything.
- As you talk, say the doing you are working on, out loud, to your partner.
- If you get stuck, this is another good time to "say the doing."

So, as you see, I am asking you to do a true, free association directed at your partner. First I will give you a few moments to go over your "as if" in your minds, then I will ask one of you to begin talking. As soon as I tell you to talk, start talking and fight to accomplish your doing. Also, keep saying the doing out loud. Nyle, you might say "Tell me the truth!" and Miryame, you could simply say, "Back off!" This will remind you what you are fighting for, and it will help get the doing into your body. After working this exercise for a while, you won't have to say the doing anymore.

It is also very important that you do not try to figure out how to "demand the truth" or how to "back her off" — simply do the other things I have just told you, and you will discover how to do it, in the doing of it. I'll say that again. You mustn't stop to try and figure out how to do the doing. You must put your attention on your partner and do all of the things I just listed. When you do this, *you will discover how to do it, in the doing of it!*

One more time, here are your instructions. Once you begin:

- Keep talking, do not stop.
- No pauses – keep talking.
- If you don't have the words, keep talking.
- Allow yourself to say whatever comes out of your mouth.
- Do not censor anything.
- As you talk, say the doing you are working on, to your partner.
- If you get stuck, this is another good time to "say the doing."

Larry: Let's do the exercise. I want you both to close your eyes, go over your circumstances in your mind, then open your eyes and look at your partner.

(Nyle and Miryame close their eyes, and after about a minute, they open their eyes and look at each other.)

Larry: Nyle, demand the truth from Edna.

Nyle: *(Immediately starts talking to Miryame.)* How can you keep this from me Edna, what kind of person are you, this is not fair, it's just not fair...

Larry: *(Speaking rapidly, with great urgency!)* Don't reason with her, demand the truth! Say it, "Tell me the truth Edna!"

Nyle: Tell me the truth Edna, you tell me the truth, I have always trusted you and I know your parents are up to no good and I know that you know exactly what they are doing and I don't think...

Larry: (*Demanding Nyle to take action!*) Nyle! There's no time to explain yourself, get the truth now!

Nyle: You tell me the truth Edna! Tell me the truth, I see you hiding it from me and I have to know what they are doing, this is going to kill my mother if it's true and you have to tell me if it's really going to happen! (*Nyle is growing more impassioned with each word out of her mouth.*) You have to tell me right now, open that mouth and tell me the truth Edna!

Larry: (*Yelling in.*) Miryame, talk to Teri, back her off!

Miryame: You back off, I can't say anything... (*Miryame pauses.*)

Larry: Keep talking. If you get stuck, say the doing, "Back off!"

Miryame: Back off! Leave me alone, I can't help you, I just can't, why do you want to treat me like this, why are you pushing...

Larry: No, no questions! Back her off!

Miryame: I don't have what you want to hear Teri so leave me alone and stop pressuring me, stop pressuring me, back off, just back off! It's too dangerous to say anything and I can't do it, so stop attacking me!

Larry: Nyle, get the truth!

Nyle: I have to know, this will kill my mother if it's true, you tell me right now, RIGHT NOW! I won't stop until I get the truth from you...

Larry: Miryame: Back her off!

Miryame: Back off! Don't pressure me, I can't help you, It would kill me, stop pressuring me, back off and leave me alone!

Larry: Nyle, get the truth!

Nyle: Don't you dare hold this back from me, you give me the answer right now and tell me what they are going to do. I want the truth Edna, you tell me now, I can't waste time with you, I need to know, you tell me!

Larry: Miryame: Back her off!

Miryame: You don't understand that I can't say anything so quit attacking me, you stop it now! Back off, you are hurting me with this and I want you to stop!

Larry: Nyle, go!

Nyle: I have to know now, you tell me now!

Larry: Miryame go!

Miryame: Stop! Just stop! Can't you see it's impossible. Back the hell off!

Larry: Nyle, go!

Nyle: Tell me!

Larry: Miryame go!

Miryame: Back the hell off!

Larry: ALL RIGHT! Let's stop here. Very nice work, both of you. *(Larry turns to the class and to you, the reader.)* Tell me, what did you see happen as Nyle and Miryame worked.

Tali: When Nyle and Miryame began the exercise, the doing was like an idea, they were talking but I·felt like they didn't really know what they were doing. And then, you helped them move past explaining themselves or questioning the other person and, wow, as they started to actually do the doing, I could see the doing begin to actually live in them.

Larry: Did they stop to figure out how to do the doing?

D'Vorah: No, they never really stopped because you kept pushing them to continue. And what I loved was that because they couldn't pause to think, they started to get out of their own way and the doing took over. It was like, suddenly, the doing clicked in and everything in their behavior was trying to accomplish that thing. That was cool!

Larry: That's right. If you do this exercise, in the manner Nyle, Miryame, and I just worked through it, the doing clicks in! It begins to live in you. When this happens, you not only know "what" you are doing, now, you really know "why" you are doing it! I'll tell ya, that's exciting! (*Larry turns back to Miryame and Nyle.*) I want you both to continue this exercise at home and learn the words of this beat. On Wednesday night, I will teach you the next step of this exercise. That's right folks, today's work was step one in personalizing the doing. See you on Wednesday.

(*Flash forward to Wednesday night, we are back where it's happening, Studio Five. Larry is in front of the group.*)

Larry: I have to share something with all of you. Sometimes you come across a talent so huge that the world stops for you. That happened to me between last class and tonight. Braeson gave me a CD to listen to called "Songbird" by a singer named, Eva Cassidy. Listening to her sing is an intensely exquisite experience. Well, no words can really give justice to this kind of thing. I know you all know what I mean. As wonderful as it is to hear her, it is equally heartbreaking because Eva died much too soon. I hope you will all listen to her. In her singing, she lives all the values we are striving so hard to attain here in class.

All right, let's continue with the work on personalizing the doing. Nyle and Miryame, would you come back up to work please?

(*Nyle and Miryame come up to the front of class and sit facing each other.*)

Larry: Have you both learned the words?

Miryame: Yes, we have learned the words and we did a number of line rehearsals together, so we know them really well now.

Larry: Good.

Nyle: And we practiced the exercise with our doings.

Larry: Okay, now I am going to have you do that exercise again, in the same way — with one addition. After you start talking to each other and when I see you get grounded in the doings, I will say, "Go to the words." When I tell you to do that, begin the words from the script, allowing the words from the script to ride on whatever is happening in that moment. Does that make sense?

Miryame. You mean that you will tell us when to switch from our own story to the words from the play?

Larry: Yes. And allow the words to ride on whatever is going on with you in that moment. Then, as you go through the beat, don't try to "hold on to" the doing. Simply work off of your partner and see where, working off of your partner, leads you.

Miryame: Yes, I understand that.

Larry: Good, let's begin. When you hear me say your name, you start talking. And, when I tell you to "Go to the words," begin to use the words from the script. At different points during the exercise, I will take you back and forth — your own story, the words of the script, your own story, the words of the script. Here we go.

Close your eyes, remind yourself of your imaginary circumstances, and when you are both ready, get what you need from the other person. Nyle, "Demand the truth" and Miryame, "Back her off."

(*Nyle and Miryame prepare with their eyes closed. When they open them, Nyle immediately begins speaking...*)

Nyle: Tell me the truth Edna! I have to know, I have to know what they are doing, this will destroy us, you tell me if it's really going to happen!

Larry: Miryame!

Miryame: I can't say anything, stop attacking me, you stop it now! Back off, you are hurting me, I want you to stop!

Larry: Nyle!

Nyle: I have to know, you tell me now!

Larry: Miryame!

Miryame: Stop! It's impossible. Back the hell off!

Larry: Nyle!

Nyle: Tell me!

Larry: Miryame go!

Miryame: Back the hell off!

Larry: Nyle, Go to the words!

Nyle: Arabella, you know something you're not telling me.

Miryame: No, I don't. Honest, Wilma...

Nyle: You do. Look at me, Arabella...

Miryame: I don't know anything. I swear...

Nyle: You do. I thought you were my friend.

Miryame: I am. I am.

Nyle: Well, then why don't you tell me?

Miryame: Because I promised not to.

Nyle: Why?

Miryame: Well... I...

Larry: Nyle, go back to your story.

Nyle: I have to know!

Larry: Miryame.

Miryame: It's impossible.

Larry: Nyle.

Nyle: Tell me!

Larry: Miryame.

Miryame: Please, back off.

Larry: Nyle, Go to "What is it? Arabella, please tell me."

Nyle: What is it? Arabella, please tell me.

Miryame: Well... Will you never say I told you?

Nyle: I swear.

Miryame: Well, I didn't tell you before because in all the excitement in telling you I wasn't going to Hollywood and your saying you weren't going, I forgot about it... until that man came...

Nyle. What is it, Arabella? What is it?

Miryame: Well, I heard my daddy tell my mother that Mr. Lester had taken out a license to marry Mrs. Leighton.

Nyle: Oh, well. That doesn't surprise me too much. I've been looking for that to happen.

Miryame: But that isn't all, Wilma...

Larry: Nyle, go back to your story.

Nyle: I want the truth!

Larry: Miryame.

Miryame: Don't attack me.

Larry: Nyle.

Nyle: Tell me!

Larry: Miryame.

Miryame: Please, please.

Larry: Nyle, Go to the words, "What else?"

Nyle: What else?

Miryame: Well...

Nyle: What else?

Miryame: Well...

Nyle: What else, Arabella? What else?...

Miryame: Well... My daddy heard that your daddy had put this house up for sale...

Nyle: I don't believe you...

Miryame: That's what he said, Wilma... I... He said Mr. Lester came to him and wanted to know if he wanted to buy it...

Larry: Okay, good! Good work you two! That was terrific! Because the readers are not here in class with us and could not actually see the work that Nyle and Miryame just did, would someone tell them what it was like to watch Nyle and Miryame.

Celina: I will. I could feel the deep need they each had to get the other person to give them what they wanted. And when they went to the words, the scene took on such incredible importance for both of them. Also, because we are in class and know what the doings are, I could see them actually fighting for those things in each moment, using the words of the play to accomplish their doings. It was also exciting to see how they never lost sense of the doing – even though the ways they did it changed.

Daryl: Yeah, you talked about adjustments that are a result of working off the other person. Even though they never gave up their doings, I could really see them adjusting to each other along the way depending on what they were getting from each other.

Larry: That's an important point. Some actors sit down and give every line in the play a different doing. Whew, That's a lot of work! Not only is it unnecessary, it will bog you down to the point of paralysis! You see, the doing may last for some time but the way you do it will keep changing because of the other person. These are the "adjustments." This is great to know when you break the play down into beats. You must ask yourself, is this really a new beat or is it actually the same doing with a new adjustment? Sometimes, you can only discover this in rehearsals with your partners.

(*Larry turns back to Miryame and Nyle.*)

Larry: Next my dears, I want you to do this exercise a number of times at home. Then, before next class, I want you to do it in the following way:

- Sit down to work.
- Close your eyes and get in touch with your circumstances.
- Say the doing to yourself.
- Then start the beat using only the words of the play.

Larry: Do this a few times before our next class. Good work today! See you all on Monday. (*Larry leaves Studio Five and gives his full attention back to you, the reader.*)

So what will happen next with Nyle and Miryame and this beat they have been working on?

Well, if they rehearse the exercise as we did today, they will continue to "plant" the personal meaning of their doings into the "soil" of the words. And, ultimately, the words of the play, on their own, will inject them right into the meaning of the doing, with no effort on Nyle or Miryame's part. In this way, as we have learned in previous exercises, the audience will see Wilma and Arabella fighting to achieve something that is vital to them. At the same time, the audience will experience the "unstated," gut-level meaning, that Nyle and Miryame have brought to what they are doing. This is where acting in live theater or in the movies, or anywhere else, becomes extraordinary!

Now, as I have said with other elements of our work on interpretation, the more you do these exercises, the more you will know when you need them. Sometimes, you can listen to a song and you will find an important clue there. Or you might see a mother hugging her baby and that becomes your inspiration. Truly, there are many ways in!

Boy, I have given you a lot to chew on.

Here's my suggestion.

If you are a young woman, take the scene in Chapter Two, get yourself a partner and work through the scene using everything you have learned here in the book. By the way, you don't need to be a teenager to do this scene. I have worked on it with many students in their twenties who have had the time of their lives with this material. For everybody else, find a scene you would love to work on and put into practice all of the lessons in this book. Take your time and be thorough. Then, one step at a time, slowly and meticulously, beat by beat, you will learn what it really is, to build a role.

Artists must be sacrificed to their art.
Like bees, they must put their lives into the sting they give.
Ralph Waldo Emerson

c h a p t e r   e l e v e n

wrapping up the series!

So, in concluding this book, I realize that there is something I have said in various ways throughout these pages, that I want to say to you one more time.

Everything we have done together in this book, all of it, are things you must incorporate into your homework and rehearsal technique.

You see, when that curtain goes up on opening night, or the camera begins to roll, you must give yourself over to your acting partners. Together with them, you get to go on the ride of your life. In this way, you are truly having an improvisation on stage, because when you are fully in the present, what's coming up next will be a surprise. And, when you are really available to your partners, no two shows will ever be the same. And this is what we want; this, in fact, is the life of the play! Do you get that? This is what makes every night, the first time. And, isn't that your job? Isn't it your job to live out the events of the play as if it was the first time they have ever happened to you? Yes it is. That's what the audience must believe and that's why you get paid the big bucks!

But wait. That doesn't mean all the meticulous work you have done goes away. No! If you have done your homework well, all the things you have personalized, all of the choices you have made will tell the story of the play "through you." The life you have invested will be enriched and deepened with each performance. This, my friends, is true joy.

What's next for you?

Here's one thing I know: If you are going to continue to seek the acting values I have been sharing with you in my four books on the Meisner approach, it's gotta be tasty to you; it simply has to be appetizing and real juicy. I do hope, among other things, that you discovered something about your own, deeply personal longing when it comes to acting and that you now have a clear sense of the kind of actor you will strive to be.

Of course, I hope you have actually worked your way through all four books because, as I have said many times, the true value in these books is in the doing of them. These books were never meant for the critics. And they were not meant for the casual reader. Both groups may enjoy them or not, but they will never know the absolute ecstasy this work offers to those who put it into practice.

Speaking about putting the work into practice, this year I was fortunate to see one of those rare, exquisite performances that absolutely glow and pulsate with life, that take ahold of your soul and won't let go. The performance was by the actress Frances Sternhagen and the play was *The Exact Center of the Universe* (a play published by Smith and Kraus). I wanted to mention Frances's performance to you, not only because she happened to study with Sandy, but because in whatever role I have seen her play over the years, she is the most beautiful example of everything we have worked on in these four books. Frances brings to the stage a character rich in personal meaning and humanity, vibrantly alive in the present, thrillingly relentless, and utterly simple. It isn't often that a performance stays with me for months and months, but I can easily drift into the pleasure of recalling so many delicious moments Frances had with her partners on stage. Oh, if only you could have witnessed Frances as the center of that particular universe!

I want you to know that this series of books came from my own deep-seated need to share with you a gift given to me that transformed my life, the gift I received from Sanford Meisner and my other teachers: Suzanne Shepherd, Phil Gushee, and William Alderson. There are a few other people who have made my writing of these books a possibility and who have been a crucial source of inspiration to me throughout the writing of them – Horton Foote, Stewart Stern, and April Shawhan. I am deeply grateful to all of these wonderful artists and mentors.

I have to tell you that having my books out there in the world has been a wonderful gift. I have received letters from every part of the planet, from people who tell me that they have found the books inspiring and useful. Well, I am thrilled that you are being inspired. Even more so, I love that you are finding my books useful! That means the world to me. You mean the world to me! And that's what got me into this book business to begin with. So please, continue writing to me, e-mailing me, and logging onto my website:

www.actorscraft.com, and let me know how the work is going. You will find all my contact information in my biography.

I thank you for your attention. And I wish you good health and a life rich in love and the warmth of family, friends, and like-minded artists who will encourage your talents in profound ways.

Be well, my friends!

Love, Larry

The Author

Larry Silverberg, author of the four-volume series *The Sanford Meisner Approach: An Actors Workbook,* the two-volume series *The Actors Guide To Qualified Acting Coaches,* and *Loving To Audition,* is a graduate of the Neighborhood Playhouse School of Theatre where he studied with master acting teacher Sanford Meisner. Since then he has worked professionally as an actor and director across the United States and in Canada. Most recently, Larry received the Seattle Critic's Association "Stellar Acting Award" for his portrayal of "Teach" in the Belltown Theatre Center production of David Mamet's *American Buffalo.*

Larry also teaches his professional intensive: the "Meisner Actor's Training Program" in New York City, and he has taught master classes in the Meisner work at universities, high schools, and acting studios in many parts of the world. If you are interested in studying with Larry or having him teach his visiting workshops at your school, please contact him by telephone at (212) 462-3005 or write to him care of Smith and Kraus Publishers, PO Box 127, Lyme, NH 03768. His website address is www.actorscraft.com.

The
SANFORD MEISNER
Approach

The best-selling workbook series that opens the door to Meisner's Approach

"Here, Silverberg, who was a student of the master teacher, presents a workbook for actors that will prove useful, regardless of how familiar the reader is with Meisner's methods. Silverberg's writing is concise and insightful throughout and makes the technique accessible to any committed student." —*Library Journal*

"For serious theatre students, this book could be highly influential in laying a foundation for their acting careers."
—*Voice of Youth Advocates*

Both books include specific exercises from the Method.

WORKBOOK ONE: AN ACTOR'S WORKBOOK
ISBN 1-880399-77-6, 176 pages, $12.95

WORKBOOK TWO: EMOTIONAL FREEDOM
ISBN 1-57525-074-8, 116 pages, $14.95

WORKBOOK THREE: TACKLING THE TEXT
ISBN 1-57525-130-2, 132 pages, $14.95

Published by Smith and Kraus
*Available at your local bookstore
or call 1.800.895.4331*

The Actor's Guide
to Qualified Acting Coaches

by Larry Silverberg

VOLUME I: NEW YORK
VOLUME II: LOS ANGELES

Finding the right acting coaches to work with, those you can trust and learn from, those who are best suited for your own skill levels and career goals, can be an overwhelming undertaking. Now there's help!

The Actor's Guide to Qualified Acting Coaches *will lead you to the finest acting teachers in New York and Los Angeles through penetrating interviews with teachers and their students.*

NEW YORK VOLUME
ISBN 1-57525-009-8
160 pages $11.95

LOS ANGELES VOLUME
ISBN 1-57525-010-1
160 pages $11.95

Published by Smith and Kraus
*Available at your local bookstore
or call 1.800.895.4331*

Loving to Audition

The Audition Workbook for Actors
by Larry Silverberg

"A valuable, adventurous,
and enthusiastic entrée into the little defined
world of auditioning."

Allan Miller, actor, director, teacher, and author

"Acting coach Larry Silverberg takes two monologues and pro-
ceeds for 147 pages to dissect every word, every possible
layer of meaning, every possible angle of approach, to show
how a master actor would interpret the speeches at an audition. Silverberg supplies so many techniques for climbing
inside the brief texts that any actor with the presence of mind
to recall a tenth of them in the heat of a real-life audition
would have the basis for ample calm confidence. This is a
really useful guide for absorbing text quickly — whether for
performer or audience."

*Drama, Dance, and Theater Editor's
Recommended Book, Amazon.com*

includes specific exercises

LOVING TO AUDITION
ISBN 1-57525-007-1, 144 pages, $15.95

Published by Smith and Kraus
*Available at your local bookstore
or call 1.800.895.4331*